A BROKEN BADGE HEALED?

ENDORSEMENT PAGE

"Frederic Donner's approach to cancer and the bureau [was much] like his approach to SWAT operations: address the problems head on, fight for what is right and know that second place can cost your life. He is a complex individual; mixing undercover "criminal" looks and personality, with law degree analysis and integrity. His word is never questionable. His approach to his battle with cancer and his approach to life come across in this book. Honest, level headed and insightful, Agent Donner has the real courage to speak forthrightly about the bureau and life. He candidly covers issues that everyone knows about but no one seems to fix. Like curing cancer or the bureau, there are no easy answers or quick fixes, but understanding the problems is the first step. He is always direct, usually tactful, but never acts with malice."

-Keith Tolhurst
Special Agent, Senior SWAT Team Leader, F.B.I. Phoenix

"*A Broken Badge Healed* is a worthwhile read and offers the reader a unique and authoritative perspective into the inner workings of the Federal Bureau of Investigation by one of its own. [SA] Frederic Donner dedicated 20 years of his life serving the United States of America as a member of the Special Weapons and Tactics (SWAT) and as an undercover agent targeting organized crime in the United States and abroad. His dedication to duty, honor and love of country will be greatly missed by his FBI colleagues and the citizens of our great country."

-Kenneth J. Williams
Special Agent F.B.I. Phoenix

"This book is powerful, truthful, and a provocative read regarding the inner workings of the F.B.I."

-Joseph Pistone
Retired Special Agent F.B.I. a.k.a. Donnie Brasco

Barrow Magazine - Volume 18, Issue 1, 2006
A magazine for the friends of Barrow Neurological Institute of St. Joseph's Hospital and Medical Center in Phoenix, Arizona

Gamma Knife and surgery— a winning combination

Another leading-edge technology at Barrow Neurological Institute may have saved *Fred Donner's* life. Fred, 43, was diagnosed with metastasized malignant melanoma in July 2003. The disease had spread to his brain, causing several tumors there, including one that was as big as a tangerine. Fred's neurosurgeon, Kris Smith, M.D., initially planned to operate to remove excess blood and then treat the tumors with Gamma Knife, a radiation therapy used for lesions in the brain. The surgery went as planned, but when Fred returned a week later for Gamma Knife, Dr. Smith found that the tumors were bleeding and that Fred needed a second surgery. Three weeks later, Fred underwent Gamma Knife to destroy any remaining cancer cells. A final surgery was done at the beginning of 2004 to remove scar tissue caused by the Gamma Knife procedure. "The combination of surgery and Gamma Knife treatment has extended his life," says Dr. Smith, a neurosurgeon at Barrow and director of Gamma Knife. Although Fred's case is not typical for patients with metastatic melanoma in the brain, "Gamma Knife has been effective for him," says Dr. Smith.

Gamma Knife Treatment

During treatment with Gamma Knife, the patient must wear a stereotactic (precise positioning) head frame. Fred didn't experience discomfort with the head frame or with the treatment. "You lie on a table, and gamma rays overhead are focused onto the tumor site. The treatment was not unpleasant," he says.

Fred still suffers from short-term memory loss, nerve problems, difficulty walking and some vision loss. He returns to Barrows every three months for an MRI and so far, a year after his last treatment, the tumors have not returned.

UPDATE; Six years later, Fred goes in once a year for MRI's and the tumors have not returned.

A BROKEN BADGE HEALED?

The FBI, a Special Agent, and the Cancer within Both

Frederic Donner

Copyright © 2013 by Frederic Donner.
C-RexMarketing@aol.com

Library of Congress Control Number: 2012920874
ISBN: Hardcover   978-1-4797-4605-7
           Softcover   978-1-4797-4604-0
           Ebook   978-1-4797-4606-4

All rights reserved. No part of this book may be reproduced or transmitted in any form or by any means, electronic or mechanical, including photocopying, recording, or by any information storage and retrieval system, without permission in writing from the copyright owner.

This book was printed in the United States of America.

To order additional copies of this book, contact:
Xlibris Corporation
1-888-795-4274
www.bookstore.Xlibris.com

DEDICATION

Almost every book published has a dedication page—remember that dedication to just causes is what every person should have in abundance.

This book is dedicated to Scrappy Cornelius Doo (cartoon icon Scooby Doo's nephew) because Scrappy would make an outstanding FBI agent. Scrappy is energetic and enthusiastic, and while undersized, he is confident. Scrappy is no brain surgeon, but he is willing to take on the big battles. All this is done with a sense of humor.

Good people should take on all obstacles in their fights to promote what is right. There is no excuse to do any less.

A special Thank you to the Xlibris staff including but not limited to; Sergio Lee, Faith Go, Tim Fitch, Ram Altrus who all worked so closely with my Marketing Manager, Carla Rexrode from C-Rex Marketing.

A BROKEN BADGE HEALED?

IN 1930: "I'D LIKE TO ARREST YOU, BUT I HAVE NO JURISDICTION."

IN 1940: "HANDS UP! YOU'RE UNDER ARREST."

IN 1990: "HANDS UP! YOU'RE UNDER ARREST."

IN 2012: "HANDS UP! I THINK I CAN ARREST YOU, BUT COULD YOU MAKE IT EASIER BY TELLING ME YOU'RE A TERRORIST, KNOW A TERRORIST, OR AT LEAST WATCHED A MOVIE ABOUT TERRORISTS?"

Table of Contents

Introduction / xiii
1 – Management / 1
2 – Bureaucracy and Obstruction / 13
3 – Office of Professional Responsibility / 25
4 – EEO, Racism, and Sexual Bias / 39
5 – A Zen Interlude / 51
6 – Today's "Me Generation" Employee / 53
7 – Avoid a Deadweight FBI Doom / 67
8 – Director Mueller's "New FBI" / 83
9 – Miscellaneous Areas Where the FBI Could Improve / 111
10 – Conclusions / 123
Acknowledgments / 127

Appendix 1 / 129
A Brief History of the FBI
Appendix 2 / 147
Full Text of Communications Providing Instructions on Conducting OPRs
Appendix 3 / 157
Portions of Letters Sent from the Special Agent Advisory Committee (SAAC) to the Director Concerning the Selection and Operation of Management

Introduction

It is a positive that you have this book in your hands; this means you have a concern about the FBI. Your concern may be one of curiosity, respect, fear, or loathing. As a longtime employee of the organization, I possess all these feelings, and many more.

It is very important to me that you understand my purposes in authoring this book. I am not a disgruntled employee who hates the organization and wants to embarrass it. Neither am I a bureaucratized sycophant, who wants to sing the bureau's praises to glorify the FBI's accomplishments by discussing my own personal deeds.

Most opinions (both fiction and nonfiction) concerning the FBI fall under two broad categories:

1. "Boy, the FBI is important, and wait until you hear my personal inflated, pompous role in how it works."

Or

2. "The organization is an evil, civil rights–abusing destroyer of personal freedoms."

My goal is to provide you with a very different perspective than either of those narrow views.

After I had completed writing my first book, *Zen and the Successful Horseplayer*, I knew I would someday attempt a piece on ways to help the FBI become a better organization. I wanted to provide insight to those outside the

FBI about our functions and flaws because the FBI desperately needs outside input and oversight from the people it serves.

Shortly after I had started this book, I was diagnosed with two malignant brain tumors, and as I began to undergo treatments, I realized that a refocusing of the book's contents was warranted. As I struggle with cancer, the FBI struggles with massive upheavals related to internal deficiencies and a reorganization to combat terrorism. In the summer of 2003, as I worked in Riyadh, Saudi Arabia, helping investigate terrorist groups, the terrorist tumors in my head were doing some bad actions of their own. The tumors were just as unseen yet just as potentially deadly to me as any terrorist.

What I began to realize was that there were some distinct parallels between my situation and the FBI's issues. I intend to try to educate the reader about the FBI and juxtapose and relate it to my own struggles. To understand cancer, you go to doctors, read books, and use the Internet. To understand the FBI, you talk to FBI personnel, you read books, and you look at the bureau's history. In appendix 1, I have included a brief history of the FBI. I suggest that after you read this introduction, you read appendix 1 before the rest of this book. This is particularly true if you are not familiar with the organization in historical context.

My objective is to induce good people to help the FBI be better. Just as I need dozens of doctors, nurses, oncologists, and others to help me get better, the FBI needs all the citizens of the United States to help it operate more efficiently.

"Better" is something of a key term here: there are no cancer cures. Even with successful treatment, no one beats cancer; you go into remission, you live with it, and you vigilantly monitor its existence and growth patterns to develop an appropriate strategy to combat it.

As I think of how I need to deal with cancer, I realize the above strategy is similar to how the FBI should combat terrorism and many other crimes. We do not eliminate crime; we strike at individuals and groups via intelligence activities and try to cut them out by putting criminals in jail. To do this, law enforcement monitors the expansion and movement of the larger criminal and terrorist entities. For doctors to be good physicians, they need to listen to their patients. It is not a one-way street. The employees of the FBI must serve the citizens of the United States, and to do this better, we in the FBI must listen to our citizens. For the people to accurately provide structure and guidance, they in turn must truly conceptualize where faults may exist and, conversely, where the FBI ship is on an even keel.

The FBI, or the bureau as we call it, is an infinitely dysfunctional machine, but it is not irretrievably broken. It can be fixed. For every criticism mentioned in this book, I will also provide some suggestions for rectifying mistakes and shortcomings. Ideally, my critiques will do more than that because they can allow the readers themselves to identify superior ways to correct the FBI's peccadilloes, inadequacies, and failings. One of the strongest opinions I hold is that the FBI cannot be fixed merely from within. We require an outside mandate from the people. The organization must bow its own bureaucratic desires to the decidedly greater commands of US citizens. We must listen to you, heed your criticisms, and restructure according to your demands. Most importantly, you as concerned citizens must make these demands, and you must make them soon. When enough people cry out for change and cogently explain why and how the FBI can adapt and perform the functions it was meant to complete, then change is possible. When I had brain surgery, I was forced to adapt, to learn to walk differently (particularly down the stairs), to deal with seizures, and to battle harder. I have to fight hard against an enemy I can never see. Similarly, the FBI has to work hard against terrorist groups we rarely understand.

The FBI is full of amazingly well-trained, hardworking, and brilliant employees. If given the correct guidelines and if provided with an organizational structure that encourages success, the employees of the FBI are capable of completing any mandate the US people require. I ask you to consider the issues I raise in this book, come up with solutions, and then push whatever buttons available to make the FBI remold itself. The buttons you push and the avenues of pressure are infinitely variable: speak to the FBI itself, converse with the media, or contact a congressperson or political organization. I am confident that with enough outside pressure, the quality people within the FBI will adapt.

Even from the inception, I will admit an institutional bias. While my critiques of the FBI are substantial and numerous, they still conveniently fit within the relatively slender volume you have in your hands. If I provided the deserved compliments to each person in the medical community who helped me with my cancer treatments, the good words I possess could scarcely be contained in an *A to Z World Book Encyclopedia*.

I would like you to think outside the box to develop other ways to pressure the FBI to attune itself to ideal standards the American citizen should demand. I respect you, the US citizen, more than I respect the FBI, the president, or even the Constitution. I am confident you will find thought-provoking issues within this book. You may periodically find hints of a more advisable path, but in many ways, it may be up to you to foster a workable solution.

The basic setup of this book is that each chapter will relate various areas where the FBI has serious deficiencies in structural and operational ability. Periodically, I will also relate sectors of skill and expertise (we do not always screw up). I intend to provide examples of specific lapses of competence to demonstrate many of the points I make. I will offer examples of how I am able to use my own struggles with cancer as a metaphor for how the FBI can be more effective.

That being stated, this is not a tell-all, nor is it a retribution book against specific individuals or particular organizational groups. I have no desire to embarrass any individual, and I do not reveal names of individuals who malingered, maltreated, or acted unlawfully. Periodically, I may name names to sing praises, but I will try to minimize that as well. For those of you within the organization who read this book (and I hope everyone from temporary interns to the director reads it), you will know from "whence I speak." Some of you will be able to recognize specific people and situations I discuss, but keep the names to yourself. Besides, the individual morons, losers, incompetents, and cruel folks know who they are.

One concept of the book is a critical, but constructive, review of the FBI as an institution; there will be minimal literary citations. I will not be providing an FBI text where you can locate empirical data because such volumes do not exist. As my doctors helped me, I will try to provide information the reader can use to assist the FBI. The opinions in this book are solely my own. While based on consultation and interaction with thousands of agents and nonagent employees, my conclusions are my own.

Technically, FBI agents are officially known as Special Agents. The "special" designation is to distinguish the person holding the title as having a statutory right to carry a firearm. In the law enforcement community, FBI, IRS, or DEA Special Agents commonly refer to themselves as agents, and that will be the title I will use throughout this book. Besides, "Special Agent" sounds pompous. Other common abbreviations I will utilize throughout the book include FBIHQ (FBI headquarters) to designate the FBI's management and kindred functions in Washington, DC. FBIHQ ostensibly controls how the FBI operates, and its competence, and lack thereof, will be discussed extensively in this book. Additionally, the FBI has numerous personnel overseas in LEGATS; legal attaché postings are agents who interact with other countries' law enforcement groups. These international counterparts may be the Mabahith (federal police in Saudi Arabia), the DAS (the Department of Security in Colombia, South America), or MI5 or MI6 (the equivalent of the FBI and CIA in England).

Most of this book is written from an FBI agent's perspective. My experiences with nonagent FBI employees have rarely been anything less than exemplary. Professional support employees are the true backbone of the organization. While the bureau may need a tweak here and there in the nonagent realm, it is on the agent and management side where we need the most radical change. When the doctors removed the cancer from my brain, they did not stop there. I received chemotherapy, radiation, and numerous other treatments. Health care professionals other than doctors provided many of the treatments and day-to-day care. While the majority of doctors I dealt with were fantastic, a few were disappointing. Yet every nurse, radiologist, and technician was awesome. Perhaps in our hiring of FBI agents, we need more former support employees, and doctors need more former medical technicians.

Finally, it was very important to me to write this while still a current employee. I believe strongly that being a currently employed agent lends credibility to the opinions and criticisms in this book. I am not a disgruntled former employee, and I am not hiding; due to complications from my seizures and other cancer-related issues, I have secured a medical disability retirement. I spent almost twenty years as an FBI agent in multiple offices, working drugs, Indian crimes, counterterrorism, and many other violations. I am damn proud to have been an FBI agent and to serve the American public.

Before I completed my final editing of this book, I asked a number of my coworkers to review it. I tried to locate individuals within the organization whom I respected and who were respected throughout the FBI. I received many insights that I subsequently included in the book's final format. I expected many of my coworkers to be critical of my stance that the FBI is overemphasizing counterterrorism and that the agency is on a path to self-destruction. Interestingly, after numerous reviews, only one reviewer felt I was off base. Everyone else believed, as I did, that it was folly to stress counterterrorism at the expense of all other criminal matters. Hopefully, the reviewer who was most critical of my stance will write a book that will provide his opposite perspective, and I know I will read it. The more diverse opinions the FBI obtains, the more likely it will grow and get better.

In the previous book I authored, *Zen and the Successful Horseplayer,* I often used quotes to help illustrate the importance of various issues related to Zen philosophy and its applicability to horse wagering. Periodically in this book, I will provide a quote, which may illuminate a particular theme. I will often leave it to you to decide if it is applicable or not.

> The belief in a
> supernatural source of evil
> is not necessary;
> men alone are quite capable
> of every wickedness.
> —*Joseph Conrad*

The FBI combats crime (and even evil) every day. If the bureau gets better at combating evil, the world is a safer place for you (and me). Realizing I have a very serious and likely fatal type of cancer made me want to learn the very best aggressive ways to combat it. Cancer is in some ways much like evil transformed into a disease. I instructed my doctors to identify aggressive ways to fight my cancer, and they did. Now, I ask you to help me find ways to make the FBI heal.

Thanks.

CHAPTER I

Management

Universally accepted by the agent population is that the greatest weakness in the FBI is bureau management. The weakness and incompetence are not absolute: there are countless qualified and superlative managers. Still, the problem is widespread and well known within the general FBI populace. The weaknesses are present throughout management, from the supervisory personnel to the assistant director level. However, all problems begin at the initial supervisory point. Set out below is a quotation from a Special Agent Advisory Committee (SAAC) document recommending ways to improve the selection of field supervisors:

> One of the perennial complaints of field Agents is the quality of leadership we often see. Unqualified or poorly qualified supervisors have the greatest negative impact on operations at the field level. Additionally, since promotion to field supervisor is one of the early steps in the upward path of a Bureau executive, the selection of the right candidate there has long-term implications for the FBI.
>
> While it is true that "political" skills (in the broad sense) might be increasingly important at more senior-level management positions, at the field supervisor level Special Agents are generally looking for leaders with better field experience levels, combined, of course, with some people skills.
>
> In other words, Agents would like to see a substantially greater

> *emphasis on relevant, substantive investigative experience and accomplishment in the GS-14 field supervisor selection process. We believe that going to trial as a case Agent and sweating through more than a few good cross-examinations is much more valuable in preparing a future Agent supervisor than answering telephones and writing notes at FBIHQ.*

As the above aptly identifies, without good first-line managers, we will not find and promote good upper management. More specifically, in a letter sent to the director in July 2002, the SAAC commented directly on this issue. This letter is quoted in more detail in appendix 3.

This book will discuss many similar recommendations later in this chapter. The point of my providing some of the information contemplated by the SAAC is to confirm to you that I am not the only one who is concerned with the management deficiencies. The ideal situation is to have the pyramid topped by the director, seconded by assistant directors, down all the way to supervisors. This hierarchy would operate in reverse order of competence and skill: good at the bottom, better in the middle, great toward the top, and spectacular at the pinnacle. This is not the case in the FBI today. Diagram 1 is a flowchart of the FBI management pyramid. Currently there are eleven HQ divisions, fifty-six field offices, and sixty-two international offices.

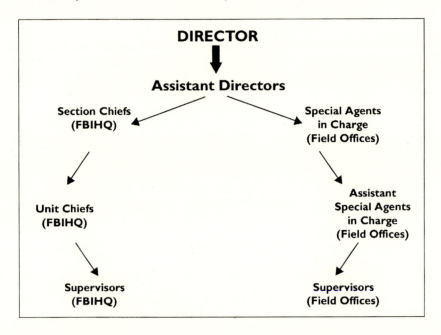

This flowchart represents far too many managers for our duties as a law enforcement and intelligence agency. If you add in a high percentage of incompetence, you have magnified the problem significantly. During my numerous hospital stays for surgery, radiation, MRIs, physical examinations, etc., I never met the hospital administrator (whom I would equate with an SAC). Yet you could feel the administrator's presence in the daily operation of the hospital staff. Important decisions were appropriately delegated to the personnel in the best position to make the call. This greatly increased the hospital's efficiency and made my hospital stay bearable. Nurses responded to calls for problems, and doctors listened to pain complaints. On one occasion, I was experiencing head pain during recovery from my brain surgery, not surprising since they removed a portion of my skull. The nurse responded to my call and agreed I probably needed a stronger painkiller. I felt much better after receiving the painkiller, but I started to hallucinate and was able to watch the walls melt together and merge. This might be fun at a Grateful Dead or Ozzy Osbourne concert, but I was concerned that maybe I was having a brain hemorrhage. I rang for the nurse again and apologized but suggested we should run a few more checks. The nurse immediately contacted help (at 1:00 a.m.), and within five minutes, I was in for an MRI and confirmation that my head was relatively okay. To date, that is the last time I have even gone close to morphine.

The point of the Grateful Dead episode is how efficiently the hospital operated during a crisis because of great employees and trust in their decisions based on instincts and training. No one felt it necessary to contact the hospital administrator. The FBI could similarly learn to delegate.

In my previous morphine example, if I had flatlined, the blame would have been quickly assumed by the intensive care unit nurse who ordered the treatment and the doctor who approved it. She told me so after the walls stopped melting into a Grateful Dead poster. The bureau could learn a lot from that ICU nurse.

With a little discourse (and hopefully a little humor), I have identified six generalized areas where deficiencies exist in bureau management:

- Competency of management is inconsistent.
- Duplication of effort exists in the field and at FBIHQ.
- Management is not held accountable for mistakes.
- Management is treated differently from other employees regarding competence and mistakes.

- Good, qualified agents do not want to become managers under the current system.
- Much of management's time is spent politicking for one's own career and not on investigative duties.

COMPETENCY OF MANAGEMENT IS INCONSISTENT

The reality of management competence is not that there are no competent managers—there are hundreds of outstanding management employees—but that competence is not universal. A few relatively minimal changes will alleviate the competency issues.

DUPLICATION OF EFFORT EXISTS IN THE FIELD AND AT FBIHQ

There is no reason an FBIHQ supervisor needs to approve a decision that has been approved by a field supervisor. Similarly, there is no justification for a section chief to sign off on a decision approved by a field SAC. This duplication and institutional distrust of one individual making a major decision and subsequently being second-guessed by someone at the same level is a great weakness in FBI management today. It also offers every decision maker a finger-pointing opportunity if it fails.

MANAGEMENT IS NOT HELD ACCOUNTABLE FOR MISTAKES

If something bad happens in a case, the field supervisor can merely say, "Well, HQ approved it!" And the HQ supervisor can state, "Well, the field supervisor was there on scene. The responsibility lies there!" Supervisors do not wish to be held accountable for what might happen.

MANAGEMENT IS TREATED DIFFERENTLY FROM OTHER BUREAU EMPLOYEES REGARDING COMPETENCE AND MISTAKES

One would expect that as an employee is promoted within the organization, the employee would be held to higher standards of competence and accountability for misjudgment. Unfortunately, this is untrue in the FBI. Once inside the circle of management and now knowing the secret handshake, a manager is often protected from scrutiny pertaining to mistakes that would get a mere agent in serious trouble. As an example, an SAC in Miami was paid a monthly retention bonus while a majority of his office perceived him to be incompetent.

Incidents similar to this occur because no one is likely to scrutinize the competence of an SAC. If complaints are made, they are covered up because the people rating and judging an SAC are people who may later work for him. If they come down too hard on him, he may later make their jobs hell.

Managers are routinely accused of things that are subsequently shoved under the rug. A supervisor in Phoenix facing an EEO issue and numerous complaints from his employees was never demoted to agent. Instead, he was reassigned five times to hide his deficiencies.

The joke among agents is that when one enters management, they go back to Quantico for training and return with a new attitude and a lobotomy scar. Now while I myself have a hell of a scar where surgeons removed my brain tumors, it is thankfully in the wrong place to be a lobotomy marking. Another joke is that those in management are Gumby (like the green bendable toy) since their spine was removed. Others argue that, at least for the male management, the cutting and removal took place a bit lower than the spine.

GOOD, QUALIFIED AGENTS DO NOT WANT TO BECOME MANAGERS UNDER THE CURRENT SYSTEM

The universally held belief in the FBI is that there are two good jobs in the bureau—street agent and SAC. These are the only positions where one has the ability to make independent decisions. Additionally, there are a number of disincentives to entering management. The relatively minimal pay increase is offset by a cost-of-living increase. If someone aspires to upper management, relocations around the country (and the world) are very difficult on a family. An SAC I very much respect once commented to me that I was smart to have remained a street agent. He knew I was working hard but that I was also having some fun. He, conversely, was working hard, dealing with OPRs, employee whining, and ridiculous inquiries from HQ. Perhaps the definition of good jobs should be narrowed to agent only.

MUCH OF MANAGEMENT'S TIME IS SPENT POLITICKING FOR ONE'S OWN CAREER AND NOT ON INVESTIGATIVE DUTIES

FBI management has some of the best ass-kissing politicians I have ever observed. Butt-kissing is an art form at HQ, and without those skills (which are honed to razor-like sharpness there), no one moves up the chain. As an example, employees with valuable international experience who have worked in legal attachés (the FBI's international offices) often have a difficult time being promoted to a supervisory job in the United States because they have not been to HQ to develop their political connections.

The ranks of management are replete with Blue Flamers, unqualified managers who rocket-ship up the organizational ladder with flames flaring out their butts, who never learned to do their job before promotion. Consider the following quote by author Alin Austin:

> To really know what success means,
> earn it.
> Don't rely on some elevator to get
> you there.
> The easiest lessons to remember are the
> ones you learned the hard way.
> The higher the floor you want to
> reach, the more important it is to take the stairs.

We in the FBI need to take Austin's quote to heart when assessing our management structure. Take your time, learn your job, get competent, and have fun along the way. An old supervisor of mine once commented to me, "You have a job, I have a career." He may have been correct, but I like working. We need more managers who are willing to learn the skills to be a good leader. We need fewer ass-kissers and more workers.

> I see no virtues
> where I smell no sweat.
> —*Francis Quarles*

These problems can be quickly remedied with some simple changes and alterations of focus. Before I provide my recommendations to solve management problems, I would like to comment that the FBI does have some competent and outstanding management, but it is just a matter of luck. If 75 percent of agents who choose to go into management are only minimally competent or ill prepared, that still leaves 25 percent who have it together. When you are working for one of those in the 25 percent, life can be good, but as an organization, we have a duty to improve those statistics. Let us retain the 25 percent and get some of the best employees involved in the lower rungs of management so the future brightens.

Here is how:

SOLUTIONS TO MANAGEMENT ISSUES

Require Passing a Relevant Test Prior to Being Promoted

If the testing were job pertinent, passing of the test would be a good indicator of real-life success after the promotion. While I will frequently criticize the FBI, I comment here that within the last few years, it has in fact attempted new testing systems, which are job specific and are supposedly required before a promotion. They are specific to the level one would seek next. If you were currently an agent, you would take the supervisor test; a supervisor would take the ASAC test, etc. I commend the FBI for the effort in this much-needed step. I have had a number of friends take the various tests (which involve written work and interactive practical problems) who have commented on the legitimate pertinence and value of the tests. However, in the Phoenix office, I am aware that seven of the more productive agents in the office were among those deemed unsatisfactory. Additionally, another agent who took the test believed that a major weakness in the process is that some of the role players in the practical problems were non-FBI employees. All testers and raters should be current or retired agents.

While I praise the FBI for a positive move, I believe it may become a rubber stamp everyone will pass. The reason is that if a large percentage of people fail the test, some group that alleges discriminative impact may halt the process. The process may be like chemotherapy, in very advanced stages, in a cancer patient—painful, unpleasant, and unlikely to succeed. I believe there are more effective and efficient ways to select management than testing, yet as an initial weeding-out process, testing is conceivably a good first step if implemented correctly.

No More Blue Flamers

This is an easy-to-initiate rule: no agent would be eligible to become a supervisor (either in the field or HQ) until a certain time had elapsed. A minimum of seven to ten years as a field agent would be required before promotion. This simple, basic step would eliminate from management those employees who have not functioned successfully as field agents.

> The highest proof of virtue
> is to possess boundless power
> without abusing it.
> —*Thomas B. Macaulay*

Management Should Not Be Elective

Under our current management structure, employees ask to be promoted by merely raising their hand. If we operated as a successful business, an employee's direct superior (the ASAC or unit chief) would select a supervisor, and the SAC would select the ASAC. There would be no more career boards—the FBI's supposed independent groups that select managers. The obvious ancillary rule is to hold the ASAC directly responsible for the competence and work product of the supervisors he or she selects. If the SAC chooses to select a champion bootlicker who is incompetent, the SAC will subsequently downgrade the ASAC's rating due to his or her poor judgment. Wow! Is that not a simple solution—imposed accountability, which all private companies strive for and many achieve?

Everyone reading this who works in the FBI is thinking, great idea, but no one will apply for "bad jobs" (supervisor at HQ, LEGAT Saudi Arabia, etc.). Remember, the subtitle of this section is "Management Should Not Be Elective." This cuts both ways: while upper management is accountable for their underling's actions, they are also able to choose whomever they desire to fill these positions. No one offered a promotion could refuse (like the Mafia). If selected by a superior for promotion, you would be required to go. It would not be relevant whether the promotion was back to HQ or internally in a field office. Of course, if extenuating circumstances exist, an agent would have the opportunity to discuss with his or her superior why a promotion might not be appropriate at the time. Still, the bottom line is that the superior's decision is final, and if he or she says "Go," you go! Many agents believe it would be preferable to create better incentives (read "higher pay") for managers than to create a non-elective management structure. However, I feel that while incentives for managers should be raised, forced management is necessary.

This would be a radical concept in the FBI, but a great step toward accountability and competence. Additionally, this change would immediately solve the issue of good agents not entering management because the choice would no longer rest with the agent. Further, this procedure would eliminate the stigma sometimes attached with going into management, because if you were not in management by ten years or so, it would be clear your capabilities would be questionable. Finally, this type of system would ensure that outstanding employees filled the less-desirable jobs.

I was fortunate to have worked a temporary duty assignment in Riyadh, Saudi Arabia, just before the diagnosis of cancer. With the possible exception of some of my undercover assignments, my Riyadh duty was the best experience I had in the FBI. I worked for a LEGAT who was in temporary duty from Spain. He was tough but fair and exceptionally competent. I learned a great deal and intended to apply for the next assistant LEGAT position, which opened in Saudi Arabia. Unfortunately, I became sick before I was able to apply. The point of my Riyadh digression is that while I was there, the FBI had significant difficulty filling the full-time LEGAT position. No one wanted to transfer to and live in Saudi Arabia. Actually, Saudi is a pretty nice place, but much more importantly, it is an important locale in the war against terrorism and one of the primary bases of al-Qaeda. The FBI needs to be sending a shining star to this integral and drastically important LEGAT job, whether he (and it needs to be a male) wants to transfer or not.

SACs demonstrate a complete affirmation of how accountability does, even now, seem to work in the FBI. These heads of individual offices tend to be very competent, driven, and often, even innovative. I have worked for approximately a dozen SACs, and every single one was pretty damn good. They each had their own personal styles, and some employees did not like them as individuals, but competence was never an issue. No one has to like or adore their superiors, but they should respect them. I was fortunate to have respected all my SACs and am proud to have worked for and interacted with all of them. The director selects SACs, and the director will be certain he does not, for example, send some loser to represent the FBI in any state. The director does not want a telephone call or message from a police chief indicating that an SAC is a dumb ass. For this reason, SACs tend to be very competent. This is not necessarily true of their section chief counterparts at FBIHQ. This dichotomy occurs because the HQ section chiefs have direct oversight by assistant directors and the like. SACs are basically on their own, and the director ensures quality in the individuals filling these important jobs. Even now, career boards are merely rubber-stamping the SAC selections made by the director. The current quality at the SAC positions is a perfect example of why direct accountability and selection of underlings should be handled not by career boards but by the immediate superior.

Demotion Should Be Available for Poor Performers

In most business environments, if an employee does a poor job, he or she is dismissed or demoted. Due to legal issues related to government employment, it might be difficult to fire poorly performing FBI managers, yet it is not required that they be retained in a management job. The current FBI method for eliminating bad managers is to promote them to a higher position, out of immediate view.

This ludicrous practice of taking a bad supervisor and promoting him or her to a unit chief job at HQ must be stopped, and poor supervisors should be demoted to agent where there is additional oversight on their poor performance. If due to legal constraints we are unable to cut the manager's pay to the agent level, the bureau should tolerate this. Maintaining bad managers in crucial positions is unconscionable if there is a vehicle to demote them. Extra money spent from demoted management will be offset by replacing the position with decision makers that are competent and have more experience.

Eliminate All FBI Headquarters Supervisors

In chemotherapy treatments, they have what are called clinical trials. In essence, these clinical trials are important medical studies that test new therapies and drugs. In chemotherapy clinical trials, these trials, or tests, are generally double-blind studies (i.e., neither the trial administrators nor the patients know who gets what drug). One group gets the normal chemo treatment, and the other group gets the normal treatment in addition to the drug or therapy being tested in the trial. Both groups of patients receive the standardized therapy, and one group tests a new potentially improved treatment. Then the patient groups are monitored to determine if one treatment does better or has more side effects. The idea is that as the doctors try to help the individual, they also identify new treatments that may help (or even possibly cure) future cancer patients. Doctors must make risky calls every day. Based on training, judgment, and consultation with the individual patient, they may recommend an unusual treatment or perhaps no treatment at all. When you meet with these doctors, you can see that they genuinely care, but sometimes, they have little encouraging information to pass on to the patient.

Originally, my doctors believed that with radiation therapy and chemo, they would be able to stop the tumors in my brain. However, after subsequent analysis and hemorrhaging, it was determined this was not likely. My doctors recommended brain surgery immediately to remove the tumors. I agreed even though the potential for serious side effects (blindness, impaired motor skills, and decreased mental ability) were significant. After the surgery, I was a blithering idiot for a few weeks. I slurred words, could not remember things, wrote like a ten-year-old, stumbled when I walked, and could not see in my lower right-hand vision quadrant. Shortly thereafter, I suffered grand mal seizures. Fun stuff, huh, but actually, the doctors were correct. After six months, most of my vision was back, I could run a few miles at a time, my memory was fairly intact, and I wrote this book!

My doctors recommended a risky procedure that, while not pleasant, appears to have paid off.

> There are two worlds:
> the world we can measure with line and rule,
> and the world that we feel with our
> hearts and imagination.
> —Leigh Hunt

My risky recommendation to address the deficiency in some managers and the massive duplication between FBIHQ and the field is simple but quite radical. Eliminate all FBIHQ supervisory positions. If the field supervisor can approve it, and since he or she has the firsthand knowledge, why send it to HQ for someone at the same level to second-guess? If it needs a higher approval level, send it to the ASAC in the field or the unit chief at HQ. Some in the bureau argue that HQ experience broadens an agent's perspective. This may be accurate (though I would address this via rotation and transfers to other field offices), but it is upper management that would benefit most from a broadened view. The field supervisors need to determine the talent and weaknesses on their squad and provide oversight to agents. ASACs, and above (in the field), and HQ need to identify broader directives and consider allocation of resources.

This radical change by eliminating HQ supervisors would also have a secondary positive benefit. Most field supervisors do not desire a lateral transfer to HQ as a supervisor. If there were no HQ supervisors, the promotional path is from field supervisor to HQ unit chief—a promotion and pay raise. Everybody gets more money, and we cut down on bureaucracy and duplication of effort. What a novel concept and a great idea.

CONCLUSION

If the simple and cost-effective solutions that are recommended in this chapter were adopted, management—which is currently the greatest weakness in the FBI—can be redeemed. As with cancer, fix what needs to be fixed most first. In my case, the brain tumors were the most urgent problem, so they were removed first via surgery. I then received radiation, followed by chemotherapy. You want to heal the entire body, but you must identify the most urgent problems and resolve them first. In the FBI, management is the urgent problem, and hopefully, utilization of some of my suggestions can help to correct the most insidious weakness of the bureau.

CHAPTER 2

Bureaucracy and Obstruction

Employees within the FBI are faced with massive bureaucracy and obstruction on a daily basis. The size of the organization itself creates much of the bureaucratic overload, and because employees need to justify their existence, additional pieces of paper are pushed through the system. Again, duplication of work in the field and FBIHQ clearly leads to additional levels of bureaucracy.

One great irony in the FBI, and in fact throughout government, is that they conduct meetings and write memoranda to discuss minimizing paperwork. The FBI was a great advocate of the Paperwork Reduction Act and switching from hard paper files to a computer-based system. The problem was, the system did not function correctly, and so the FBI continues to send out memos and electronic communications (ECs) in hard format. Why? Because it is still quicker to attach the EC to e-mail and have it subsequently printed out by each receiving party. Much of an agent's time (and virtually all of a manager's day) is spent pushing needless paper through a dysfunctional system. If you go into some of the field supervisors' offices, you see literally thousands of documents scattered about. If you examined daily duties of FBI personnel, you would see that at least 75 percent of time is spent on paperwork. That does not leave much time to conduct interviews, surveillances, and meetings. In fact, I would assert that for many employees, almost 100 percent of their time is spent completing paperwork.

Cancer patients can often be asymptomatic. In other words, the patient may show few or no symptoms. My cancer was like that. The cancer, which my doctors later determined began in my chest, showed no symptoms there, and I had no problems breathing or swallowing. It remained dormant there until sufficient cancer cells sloughed off into my bloodstream to metastasize into the brain.

In much the same way, the FBI does not always appear bureaucratic or incompetent at first glance. If you looked at operations on a daily basis, you would see us at our desks in suits and ties attempting to fight the good fight. Unfortunately, if you looked closer, you would observe many empty suits. These bureaucratized sycophants are what are called oxygen thieves. They arrive in the morning, walk around, log on the computer, push some paper around, and basically contribute nothing all day. While most organizations have several of these employees, the FBI is burdened with a large quotient of these types because the bureaucracy is so ingrained that it is much easier to hide or lie dormant.

Here is an example that demonstrates FBI bureaucracy and institutional inertia. When the FBI interviews an informant or source, one of two headings is placed on the FD-302, which records the details of the debriefing. One of two initial headings is utilized: "A source who is in a position to testify advised . . ." or "A source who is not in a position to testify advised . . ." Not very well worded, but the idea basically is that the first source could testify if needed while the second source would not be asked to testify because of safety concerns if the source was identified in court. I do not have a problem with the concept, but the verbiage is inadequate and somewhat misleading. Both sources are potentially in positions to testify (in fact, the information could be identical), yet we as the FBI are just very unlikely to ask the second source to do so. I pointed this out to a former supervisor and suggested the wording be adjusted to be more similar to the nondisclosure documents we complete with the informant when they are signed up. The wording would be similar to "The FBI will make every effort to protect the identity of the individual providing this information, though there may be situations where such disclosure may be required." This would make the documents consistent, and we would still be doing our best to protect the individual's identity. I believed it was a pretty good idea, which could forestall later problems. The supervisor dismissed the suggestion out of hand and suggested I should not make waves when no problems had occurred so far. My response was to suggest a solution to a potential problem, but my supervisor started screaming at me to stop bothering him and to get out of his office.

Trying to change something bureau-wide is seen by many as too difficult to attempt or suggest. When everything blows up, it will usually be on someone else's watch. It reminds me of the cartoon with three monkeys, one with his hands covering his eyes, one with his hands covering his ears, and the final monkey with his hands covering his mouth. To me, those three monkeys perfectly epitomize FBI bureaucracy: hear no evil, see no evil, and definitely speak no evil.

What are the most important contributors to the gridlock of bureaucracy in the FBI?

- FBIHQ is too large.
- The FBI fosters a cover-your-ass mentality.
- Field office inspections are a waste of time.
- The FBI fixes things only after they are irreparably damaged.
- Obstructing or stopping an investigation or idea is easier than promoting it.

FBIHQ IS TOO LARGE

A large percentage of FBI employees work either at headquarters (known to all FBI employees as HQ), Quantico (the FBI's training facility), or the laboratory. This concentration of FBI employees in the Washington, DC, area is unnecessary. Employees at any company need to be located where the work will be conducted. The work of the FBI is completed in the individual field offices in the United States and in the LEGATS overseas. The farther an employee is from Washington, the more he or she understands what work is actually being done.

A briefing book is prepared for the director and his staff on a weekly basis. The information in this briefing book has become the holy grail. I have personally received telephone calls from supervisors (and above) at HQs demanding that I drop everything to obtain additional details for this weekly briefing book. The folks who demand more details could be better utilized in the field, doing interviews and coordinating investigations. At HQ, all that those employees accomplish is to push paper around and make frequent deadline demands on the field to legitimize their own existence.

> The door to virtue
> is heavy and hard to push.
> —*Chinese Proverb*

THE FBI FOSTERS A COVER-YOUR-ASS MENTALITY

Much like the three monkeys described earlier, the FBI wants to see no evil, hear no evil, and speak no evil as it relates to its own internal operations. Currently, supervisors are sent to HQ for eighteen months to two years before being sent back to the field. These employees are at the bottom of the food chain at HQ, and everyone knows crap runs downhill. No one wants to remain an HQ supervisor, and therefore, none of them make waves, which might keep them at HQ longer. Do your two years, keep your head low, cover your ass, and get out.

For this reason, I find the concept of blinkers particularly appropriate for HQ and much of the FBI. In horse racing, blinkers are used so the horse can see only forward and not to the sides. The blinkers are designed to help the horse focus. The FBI puts blinkers on its employees by counseling them not to worry about how this or that are broken, just do your job, and keep your head down in the work cubicle. However, another consequence of blinkers on some horses is that they run dull. Some horses are brighter than others, and they want to look around at the big picture. The same is true of FBI employees: some want to be innovative and solve some of the big problems.

Typically, employees closest to the problem will have the best solutions. If they are too busy watching their back, they fail to be innovative.

A courtroom is not a crucible of the truth. When an agent is preparing for a trial, he or she must try to think of other eventualities that may make it more or less likely to succeed. This thinking outside the box may lead one to an innovative strategy or at least decrease the likelihood of mistakes. A few years ago, I was testifying in a trial in Iowa, and when I spoke to the assistant United States attorney, I suggested that I physically review the drug and documentary evidence seized prior to trial. He said I did not need to worry because I would not be utilized to introduce most of the evidence. Instead, he would be introducing a smaller portion, which I had reviewed. After a brief argument, I relented (which is rare for my stubborn self). Sure as hell, he mistakenly (and accidentally) tried to have me introduce a notebook containing telephone numbers. I did not recognize it and noted the initials on it were not my own. Still, he tried to get it into evidence via my testimony. Eventually, the judge stated he would not allow the notebook into evidence. During a court recess, the prosecutor was not too happy and admitted that if we had reviewed the evidence together prior to my testimony, the problem would not have occurred. He was, in actuality, a very good prosecutor, and he won the case. The lesson is that courtrooms are not crucibles of truth, and to succeed, we need to be prepared, particularly for things that can catch an agent off guard.

The diagnosis of cancer is a shock for anyone. When we battle cancer, we must use every shred of information at our disposal. We must diligently do our homework and find alternative treatments that may be most appropriate. Nontraditional thinking in cancer treatments may include participating in clinical trials. Clinical trials involve trying new medications, which may lead to a better quality of life or, periodically, even medical breakthroughs. Most medical breakthroughs are actually advances achieved inch by inch. Similarly, successful cases in the FBI occur through diligence and following each investigative lead to its logical conclusions. Tiny steps can lead to a great increase in distance traveled if done consistently and innovatively. No one who contemplates issues from unique perspectives will ever become a cover-your-ass type. This is as true in the FBI as it is in cancer treatments.

FIELD OFFICE INSPECTIONS ARE A WASTE OF TIME

Approximately every two to three years, the inspection staff reviews each field office, LEGAT, or headquarters division. The procedure is a farce, involving collusion between those being inspected and those conducting the inspection. Beyond the undeniable conclusion that both sides know what the answers are, it does not mean a damn thing. The reams of paper consisting of interrogatories, responses, and counter responses are mind-boggling and literally fill rooms in FBI offices. The inspections are meaningless exercises in futility and prove that bureaucracy is firmly entrenched in the FBI. To make matters worse, between the full-scale inspections, each office does its own self-inspection to make certain it is prepared for the official inspection.

Inspections are completely one-sided. Inspections are designed to search only for negatives. The inspectors search for mistakes and errors but never look for positives. The positives of successful cases or major impacts in the community are never addressed during inspections.

One issue the inspectors review is TURK (time utilization record keeping). TURK was originally set up years ago to provide an estimation of how much time agents spent working on certain types of cases. To regulate this, agents would note on a time card that a certain percentage of their time was spent working fugitive cases, a certain percentage was spent conducting applicant matters, and so on. It made sense in that limited context. The FBI machine has now twisted TURK so blatantly that it is utilized to allocate resources for entire field offices. If the TURK numbers showed agents expended twelve "agent work years" on drugs in a given year, this would be compared with the target staffing level (TSL) for drug agents. If there was a significant discrepancy (and there always is), explanations (read "lies and excuses") would be provided to the inspectors using genuflecting and groveling. The process is a pinnacle of bureaucratic garbage. Even the people within the TURK system do not understand it, but they would tell you it is damn important whatever it is. Additionally, my understanding was that TURK was originally instituted to justify FBI allocation of resources to Congress. Yet to date, Congress has never been provided yearly TURK data.

THE FBI FIXES THINGS ONLY AFTER THEY ARE IRREPARABLY DAMAGED

My favorite description concerning the FBI is that we fix the barn door after the cows are loose and frolicking in the neighbor's pasture.

In cancer treatments, doctors do not wait until your head falls off to go after your tumors. In cancer, doctors understand the concept of "late effects." Late effects is the reality that even after a cancer is treated, it can reoccur in a different form somewhere else in the body. That is why you have follow-up treatment and monitoring even after remission. Doctors do not just do surgery and send you home without follow-up. The FBI needs to begin to monitor when it makes changes to ensure we did not cure the brain cancer by cutting off the head.

In the FBI, recent reorganization has taken place designed to make the FBI into an international terrorism-fighting agency and remove or limit our responsibilities for combating drugs, gangs, and violent crime. This is the most recent and dramatic example of making a snap decision and leaving a fairly healthy patient without a head. If we put all our FBI resources in one pot, it could seriously limit our ability to battle violent crimes, including kidnapping, drugs, and extortion.

OBSTRUCTING OR STOPPING AN INVESTIGATION OR IDEA IS EASIER THAN PROMOTING IT

In the FBI, when a new idea or means of conducting an investigation is contemplated, it is much easier to avoid the new idea than adopt it. Innovation is frowned upon. Often, particularly at HQ, cases are actively obstructed (or downplayed) because minimizing the case decreases the workload for HQ personnel. If we do not conduct the investigation, it is not necessary to work out the problems. Important cases go by the wayside because agents get tired of beating their heads against the obstruction wall.

I experienced a very dramatic example when I attempted to initiate a terrorism case against a well-known European terrorist entity. I had an informant (who was willing to testify and introduce an undercover agent) in a position to meet with an unidentified individual in the terrorist organization. Through a third-party intermediary, the source could schedule a meeting in a neutral city. The terrorist group was allegedly not only involved in selling drugs to generate income but also interested in kidnapping US citizens for ransom. While I personally did not feel the kidnappings were a high probability, I felt it important enough to send the information to both the terrorism and drug sections at HQ. I requested authority to have the source (with me acting as the undercover agent) set up a meeting with the subjects. In this way, we could identify the perpetrators in the United States and see if they were seriously considering kidnappings. I believed the idea was logical and straightforward: conduct a meeting, attempt to fully identify the subjects, get some contact numbers, and discuss the kidnapping issue.

Then I ran into the obstruction wall head-on. A supervisor in the terrorism section denied me authority to schedule a meeting, stating that I needed to determine exactly whom we would meet and obtain telephone numbers in the United States beforehand. He then added that in the HQ supervisor's experience, this group never attempted kidnappings within the United States. I pointed out that if I sat down with them, these questions would be resolved. Unbelievably, after numerous requests back and forth, the supervisor still said no to my simple and logical request.

Months later, a different HQ employee contacted me and said the bureau had received corroborative information of the same group conducting kidnappings. I said I would recontact the source to see if an undercover meeting was still viable. Then all hell broke loose! The first supervisor obstructionist said the matter was closed and dead and no approval would be provided unless we knew everything beforehand. She also intimated a decided lack of experience and competence on my part. I am a stubborn sort, so I withdrew my request for HQ approval for a meeting elsewhere. Instead, I advised I would attempt to schedule the meeting in Phoenix (where we could control the meeting location and other details). In this way, I no longer needed

HQ authority because I did not have to schedule the meeting in another city. Agents are now forced to devise clever ways to conduct investigations (especially undercover agents). I stopped the obstruction by going around it, but the obstructionist is still there at HQ to hamper legitimate investigations. Obstruction, even very active obstruction, is a part of every agent's day-to-day dealings. We need to fight hard to eliminate obstructionist tendencies in the FBI.

In case you are worried about that particular terrorist group kidnapping you, you may relax for now. My investigation indicated it is just drug dealing at the time. Whether I even tell HQ is a separate issue, but I will keep you (my readers) posted if they start talking kidnappings again.

> Let us recognize the beauty and power of true enthusiasm;
> and whatever we may do to enlighten ourselves or others,
> guard against checking or chilling a single
> earnest sentiment.
> —Henry Tuckerman

SOLUTIONS TO BUREAUCRATIC PROBLEMS AND OBSTRUCTION ISSUES

Think Outside the Box

The reason bureaucracies thrive is because it is easier to keep plodding along on one course than it is to change direction. The FBI should decrease bureaucratic stupidity and encourage employees throughout the agency to be innovative and brilliantly different. Individually, FBI employees are innovative and sometimes even freethinkers. The organization needs to create an environment where these types will thrive and prosper. Consider the following quote by Alin Austin:

> Don't feel like you have to choose
> between traditional choices.
> Whether to be a big fish
> in a little pond or a little fish
> in a big pond may not have
> an ounce of relevance to what
> your spirit wants to do.

> Maybe you need to be a
> speckled trout in a wilderness
> river or a flying fish in
> a tropical sea.
> Pigeon holes are for pigeons...
> not for people like you.

If we could get more FBI employees to believe that quote, we could toss much of our bureaucratic crap out the window. There are ways to foster innovative ideas, and it does not start with a suggestion box. It begins with upper management considering what employees have to say. Have the SAC get all the management together one day per month and listen to them. What can we do better? Where do we need improved skills? The questions are easy, but innovative answers are tougher to find. Then have the supervisors go back to their squads and ask the same questions of the agents and all other employees. Trust enough in your employees that you will get more by asking them how to be better than you will by forcing them to function in the traditional way.

All people have their own natural ways of creating. There is no single right way to treat cancer, nor is there a single right way to fight crime. Encourage the freethinkers, and you will be more successful. The stifling bureaucracy might just fade away, or at least, it will be somewhat diminished.

Let's Kill All the Lawyers

Okay, we are not going to literally kill them, but we do not need so many in the FBI. Bureaucracy's handmaidens are always lawsuits and legal wrangling. The FBI is a law enforcement agency. We enforce laws by piecing together cases that put criminals and terrorists in jail. As we get out of law enforcement and more into intelligence gathering and spy work, we lose our credibility as a law enforcement entity. The FBI should hire more former police officers and military, not less. The FBI's current policy is to seek out computer scientists and designated language speakers but not to hire from law enforcement and military. This is a massive mistake. While the FBI clearly needs specialists like lawyers and accountants, what is needed most are the best and brightest.

The last four full-time directors (Mueller, Freeh, Sessions, and Webster) were all lawyers. The FBI must reestablish its role as the premier law enforcement agency in the world by hiring a former major city police chief as the next director. I do feel that the FBI can handle terrorism and spies, but we need to start by being based as a law enforcement group. Our next director will likely limit bureaucratic overload more effectively if he or she is not a legal eagle. The FBI needs some lawyers, but it is unnecessary for the director to be one.

Eliminate All FBIHQ Supervisors

As mentioned in chapter 1, there is no legitimate rationale for the duplication of supervisors in the field and at FBIHQ. Additionally, to diminish bureaucracy, each division at HQ should be reduced by a least 25 percent. This could be handled by natural attrition or, more appropriately, by placing that 25 percent in LEGATS, where the real work in antiterrorism takes place. Today, the opposite of "slimming down" is occurring within the FBI. FBIHQ is being fattened with bureaucracy under the misguided idea that investigations can be run from headquarters. Headquarters staffing is greatly increasing, and this behemoth must be cut back to a manageable size.

Eliminate All Inspections at Field Offices and FBIHQ

Again, as mentioned in chapter 1, the inspections are a complete waste of time that serve no legitimate purpose. The inspection process is a collusive failure. Instead of bringing in a staff of dozens every three to four years, a single inspector should be sent to a field office to work with the supervisors and other management. This single inspector could produce a concise report of accomplishment during the time frame. A random sampling of employees should be interviewed, and that is all the scaled-down inspection would entail. The current process of large-scale inspections is the FBI bureaucracy at its very worst and should be eliminated.

CONCLUSION

The FBI is a bureaucratic nightmare of paperwork, duplication of duties, and hidebound employees who have not had an original thought in eons. Adopting even some of the suggestions for change might make significant improvements in innovation and skill, and virtually any change that reduces paperwork would be a blessing. No single solution will eliminate bureaucracy from an institution the size of the bureau, but many small steps could put us closer to the right path. When you are first diagnosed with cancer, you think, "That's it, I'm dead, it's over." This is untrue, and a cancer survivor is simply someone who is living with cancer a day at a time, one foot in front of the other. People with serious forms of cancer can outlive the mortality scales with a positive attitude. Every doctor stresses the importance of good health and an upbeat way of dealing with every day. If every day, each FBI employee tried to fix just one thing, no matter how small, imagine how we could improve and reduce bureaucratic overload.

CHAPTER 3

Office of Professional Responsibility

The FBI's Office of Professional Responsibility (OPR) is an internal entity that is akin to other law enforcement internal affairs divisions. It was set up to investigate instances where FBI employees are suspected of acting unlawfully, unethically, or both. However, the Office of Professional Responsibility is neither professional nor responsible; though I am sure they have offices somewhere (one out of three is not too bad). In OPR's case, a 33 percent batting average would greatly exceed its real-life investigative success rate. OPR is a true cancer within the FBI that must be destroyed at all costs. The entity is a true bastardization of all that is fair and equitable. If real-life criminals were treated the way OPR handles its investigative targets (FBI employees), the criminals would repeatedly be acquitted and win civil lawsuits against the bureau. OPR is held to none of the investigative standards that are required of other FBI agents during criminal, foreign counterintelligence, or terrorist investigations. OPR frequently investigates and charges innocent people; if the FBI did this as an investigative agency, we would be a disgrace to all law enforcement. OPR, as it exists today, must be cut out of the FBI, the same way cancer is cut from an otherwise healthy body. Additionally, once removed from the body of the FBI, careful monitoring must continue to ensure OPR does not metastasize into some other, more deadly form.

Virtually no one within the FBI wants to work in OPR because even if operated competently, its sole function is to punish and ruin the personal and professional careers of bureau employees. While I believe, like many others, that the FBI needs oversight of its employees, an investigation should not be brought up against an employee unless the allegations are seriously criminal in nature. When was the last time the bureau investigated a college student for cheating on his finals? Hopefully never! If it is determined that an ethical lapse occurred among our employees, that should be handled by immediate superiors and not by the incompetent mess known by the three worthless letters OPR. Conversely, if the allegations are serious, such as theft of government monies, disclosing secret or confidential information, or committing criminal activity, the investigation should be conducted by trained FBI investigators, and the perpetrators should be jailed if found guilty and not sloughed off to OPR.

OPR generally begins to initiate an investigation when it receives an allegation of misconduct (or criminal activity) by an employee. The allegation is obtained via many avenues, including but not limited to the following:

- The employee voluntarily admitting it
- Another employee or citizen reporting it
- An unrelated investigation identifying it, or
- A separate law enforcement or intelligence agency reporting it

There are numerous other ways an OPR investigation (commonly referred to internally in the FBI merely as an OPR) may be started, but the above are the most common ways. After an issue is raised, a management employee determines if an OPR case should be initiated and reports the initial issue to FBIHQ OPR to decide if an official OPR investigation should be initiated. OPR at headquarters almost always opens a case and determines if headquarters OPR investigators (agents refer to these types as the Goon Squad) should travel into the field to handle the matter. In the alternative, HQ OPR may feel the issue is not important enough for the Goon Squad, and OPR advises the field office to handle the investigation. If HQ refers the matter back to the field, any investigative results are eventually resubmitted back to FBIHQ OPR in which they have the final say as to punishment.

During the entire investigation, the employee is compelled to respond or will be summarily dismissed (i.e., fired). OPR attempts to make a distinction between administrative investigations and criminal cases, but it makes not a whit of difference because OPR may decide a criminal matter has become an administrative case or vice versa. OPR makes every decision in a way that provides OPR the most leverage. If it benefits OPR to hold the criminal charge over an employee as a threat, it will. If it benefits OPR to force the employee to make a statement by indicating it is a noncriminal matter, it will do that also.

An explanation: Until the early 1980s, OPR did not formally make a distinction between administrative and criminal OPR investigations. OPR at that time compelled all employees to answer any questions whether criminal or civil in nature. The federal courts in Cleveland bit OPR pretty hard when OPR indicted an employee on criminal charges based on his compelled statement (indicating to the employee it was only a personnel issue). The court made the government drop all charges against the employee that could have been based on his compelled (forced) statement.

The importance of these and numerous other court decisions is undeniably clear: No one can be forced to make a statement against your interests by threatening you with dismissal or imprisonment if you refuse to talk. Any such statement is inadmissible against an employee in a criminal court. OPR avoids this by including in the employee's original statement that they voluntarily provided the statement, or if compelled, the investigation was an administrative case. OPR then decides what the employee did wrong (and, in an astronomically high percentage of cases, most are confirmed as inappropriate actions by the employee); something, even minor, was done incorrectly. Then OPR decides the employee's fate. OPR either refers the matter for criminal prosecution to the United States Attorney's Office or levies an administrative sanction, which entails at minimum a letter of censure and up to ninety days without pay. For a repeat offense, OPR orders the employee to be fired.

The above paragraphs succinctly describe how OPR functions/dysfunctions. All employees (in any organization) understand that the same organization that holds out a carrot must also be capable of using the stick when employee misdeeds or unethical acts take place. Still, the incongruity of OPR reactions as related to the actual conduct is impossible to reconcile. Set out below is a quotation sent as a message from former FBI director Louis Freeh (his message was accompanied by a photograph of Abraham Lincoln). Freeh's message outlined the FBI core values, and I could not agree more with the former director. It is a shame and disgrace that the FBI's own OPR cannot approach these core values. The quote is as follows:

FBI CORE VALUES

> The strategic plan for accomplishing the FBI's mission must begin by identifying the core values which need to be preserved and defended by the FBI in performing its statutory missions. Those

values are: rigorous obedience to the Constitution of the United States; respect for the dignity of all those we protect; compassion; fairness; and uncompromising personal and institutional integrity. These values do not exhaust the many goals, which we wish to achieve, but they capsulize them as well as can be done in a few words. Our values must be fully understood, practiced, shared, vigorously defended and preserved.

Observance of these core values is our guarantee of excellence and propriety in performing the FBI's national security and criminal investigative functions. Rigorous obedience to constitutional principles ensures that individually and institutionally we always remember that constitutional guarantees are more important than the outcome of any single interview, search for evidence, or investigation. Respect for the dignity of all whom we protect reminds us to wield law enforcement powers with restraint and to recognize the natural human tendency to be corrupted by power and to become callous in its exercise. Fairness and compassion ensure that we treat everyone with the highest regard for constitutional, civil and human rights. Personal and institutional integrity reinforces each other and is owed to the Nation in exchange for the sacred trust and great authority conferred upon us.

We who enforce the Law must not merely obey it. We have an obligation to set a moral example, which those whom we protect can follow. Because the FBI's success in accomplishing its mission is directly related to the support and cooperation of those whom we protect, these core values are the fiber which holds together the vitality of our institution.

What are the greatest embarrassments within the organization of OPR, which I believe should be renamed Association of Professional Responsibility (APR)? If it were APR, employees could at least remember it by the mnemonic Abuse of Personal Rights.

When you are being investigated by OPR, it is different from being diagnosed with cancer. There is nowhere to go, and it is difficult to get positive second opinions because OPR specifically prohibits you from discussing the matter with anyone. This is merely another way to put pressure on the employee. At least cancer doctors actively encourage you to get second and third opinions. Oncologists are confident enough in their individual diagnostic abilities to have minimal fear of widely divergent second opinions. They welcome educated alternatives. Conversely, OPR fears employees discussing the investigation with others because it will likely demonstrate the inconsistencies in OPR methods. When you are being investigated by OPR, it is worse than cancer. With cancer, you get some intelligent input, but with OPR, it feels like you are in a very dark room, and the walls are closing in, and the air is slowly being sucked out.

> When we live habitually with the wicked,
> we become necessarily their victims or their disciples;
> on the contrary,
> when we associate with the virtuous,
> we form ourselves in imitation of their virtues,
> or at least lose, every day, something of our faults.
> —*Pope Agapet*

Here are the things that are wrong with OPR:

MANAGEMENT IS TREATED DIFFERENTLY WHEN INVESTIGATED BY OPR

Managers at the supervisory level and above are the only employees who conduct OPR investigations. Supervisors generally investigate agents. Supervisors are investigated by ASACs (assistant special agents in charge). HQ personnel and special teams of OPR investigators investigate ASACs and SACs (and their equivalents at FBIHQ). Though not as blatant as in the old bureau (1960s through the 1990s), management generally receives less sanctions for the same violations as agents and support personnel do. An analysis of OPR found a wide discrepancy between management punishment and lower-level employee sanctions. Recently, this gap has narrowed significantly, but it is still far from a level playing field. One of the principal reasons for this discrepancy is that if an HQ OPR investigator were investigating an SAC for misconduct, it will always be at the back of the investigator's mind that he or she may someday work for this SAC. A diminished sanction might eliminate hard feelings later. Contrary to that situation is when a supervisor or ASAC advocates sanctions on an agent: the investigator is able to punish severely because it is unlikely the agent will pass the supervisor to a higher position. Management has always been treated easier during ongoing OPRs than street-level employees, and as long as management controls OPR at the investigative level, this is unlikely to change.

THE DECISIONS RENDERED BY OPR TEND TO LACK CONSISTENCY PARTIALLY BECAUSE THE INVESTIGATORS THEMSELVES DO NOT KNOW HOW TO CONDUCT INVESTIGATIONS

When OPR investigations are delegated back to the field to be addressed, much of the quality of the investigation depends on who is assigned the case. As a principal relief supervisor, I was the secondary investigator during two relatively minor OPRs. While I felt the efforts the other supervisor and I put forth were admirable, we received little guidance from HQ OPR. They barely answered repeated inquiries from us and then disagreed with our recommendation to polygraph the employee. It seemed an easy call to request the polygraph and have the issue resolved. Our SAC agreed, but OPR said no. Being a poor decision, it also showed that even with two decent investigators (and a qualified SAC) recommending a logical course, OPR did not listen.

What happens when the investigator supervisors do not know how to conduct an investigation? OPR may likely accept their recommendation. If they will not agree with a good recommendation, it is possible they might agree to a poor choice. Finally, to confirm that many OPRs in the field are assigned to poor investigators, just ask this question: if you were an SAC and you had five top-notch supervisors who were overworked with major cases, would you assign an OPR to one of those five? Of course not. They are too busy; instead, assign it to a do-nothing slug of a supervisor.

OPR IS BASED ON A CULTURE OF LIES AND THREATS

The greatest threat OPR can hold over an employee is criminal prosecution because OPR can offer to stop the criminal charges if the employee resigns. Most employees faced with such a decision would justifiably prefer to lose their livelihood rather than their freedom. Even if the criminal case is marginal, the threat of prosecution is a big stick over an employee's head. This scenario happens in the FBI world much more often than the bureau would care to admit. Additionally, the situation is a win-win for the FBI. You rid the bureau of a bad (or good) employee while avoiding any negative media coverage of having an employee indicted on criminal charges.

I will provide a purely hypothetical example to attempt to demonstrate the above theory. Let us assume that an agent is provided $7,000 to obtain a rental vehicle. The vehicle rental is $6,000. The agent, who is awaiting a source payment approval of $1,000, utilizes the overage to pay the source. The agent waits until the $1,000 source payment is approved and then returns that money to the FBI to cover the difference. This is all right because the agent expedited the payment to the source. While agents do this type of thing frequently, if reported to OPR, OPR would surely allege either commingling of funds (mixing one case's money into another case's) or possibly theft of government property (i.e., the agent stole the $1,000). Listening to the facts, I personally see little wrong. Yet if OPR became involved, the sanctions for commingling of funds would be relatively minimal while theft of government property is criminal and might result in the agent being fired and prosecuted. It is easy to see from the above hypothetical scenario that OPR can put enormous pressure on an employee for a minimal (or even nonexistent) offense.

The other very dramatic means OPR has to promulgate its lies and misinterpretation of a situation is by prohibiting the employee from discussing the investigation with anyone except an attorney or the investigators themselves. This is garbage and in violation of the US Constitution. The exact language for both administrative and criminal inquiries can be found in appendix 2 in this book. Appendix 2 also explains how inquiries are to be conducted. How can the FBI extinguish an employee's right to free speech until the employee obtains permission from the interviewer on a routine, non-sensitive OPR? Clearly, if the OPR involves a matter of ongoing criminal activity or national security, the investigator should directly prohibit disclosure. This would be done in any normal FBI investigation. However, if the OPR investigation involves only that employee's misconduct, I believe it is unconstitutional to inhibit the employee's free speech right.

THE ADJUDICATION OF AN OPR AS RELATED TO PUNISHMENT IS WRONGLY BASED ON A PREDETERMINED SET OF FACTORS AND NOT ON A CASE-BY-CASE BASIS

OPR rigidly bases its decisions as to punishment on the so-called Douglas Factors. The issues, which are included in conducting an OPR investigation (see full text in appendix 2), are merely an excuse for not addressing each OPR separately. I find no problem in considering many (if not all) of these factors, but why make all of them a prerequisite in every OPR? Some independent thought instead of a checklist should be used. All written OPR responses I have seen merely address these issues and rarely go further. There is much more to any employee's conduct and problems than those factors.

OPR DECIDES AN EMPLOYEE'S FATE BEFORE ALL FACTS ARE IN AND CONVICTS BEFORE ANY HEARING

OPR compels employees to make statements even in criminal matters (such as "driving under the influence of alcohol" charges) then decides their fate without a hearing. Under a new policy promulgated in a letter from the Administrative Services Division dated October 24, 2003, a new policy has been set by OPR for criminal conduct. This policy, which is on page 3 of the letter, is as follows:

New Policy—Criminal Conduct

> *Should OPR find that reasonable cause exists to believe an employee has committed a crime for which a sentence of imprisonment may be imposed, a letter signed by the Deputy Assistant Director of OPR will be prepared advising the employee that he/she will be placed on indefinite suspension (without pay or duties) and the reason for such action. Reasonable cause may be established, for example, by indictment, arrest, the filing of criminal information, credible news reports of egregious acts that are detrimental to the Bureau's mission, such as murder or national security offenses, or through a judicial determination of probable cause. A warrant-less arrest alone may not be sufficient to establish reasonable cause. Separate action may be taken to suspend the employee's security clearance in connection with a criminal case. In these type of criminal conduct cases, employees will not be given the option of using leave.*

The full text of this entire administrative service letter may be found in appendix 2. The above subsection demonstrates exactly how OPR works: guilty until proven innocent. This back-ass-ward logic would be akin to telling a patient he or she will be dying of cancer before we conduct diagnostic tests or offer treatment. It goes against the very ideology of the US Constitution every FBI agent is sworn to uphold. The rules apply only when OPR wants them to; your rights as an FBI employee do not even exist.

> He who finds diamonds must grapple in mud and mire,
> because diamonds are not found in polished stones.
> They are made.
> —Henry B. Wilson

OPR GENERALLY HAS TERRIBLE EMPLOYEES AT FBI HEADQUARTERS

Virtually no one wants to work at HQ OPR. What employee would voluntarily choose an assignment where the only success is to imprison or embarrass a fellow employee? As with all management, but especially OPR, this should not be a "raise your hand" deal. If OPR is allowed to continue to exist, all employees sent there should be personally selected based on quality investigative and management experience. I cannot envision an area where a lazy, overly aggressive, or incompetent employee could do more damage to the FBI. The only qualified employee I knew at OPR was an SAC I worked for who was sent to manage OPR for a three-month temporary assignment. The SAC, who was very competent and wonderfully supportive of me during my procedures from cancer, despised every moment. She confessed to me that it was the worst assignment she ever endured in the FBI. During the same time period in which this person had been at OPR, I had been through brain surgery, radiation, spinal taps, and other miserable procedures. Still, I commiserated with this person and agreed that her previous three months were probably worse than mine were.

To get qualified people staffing OPR, the bureau must be able to hand-select supervisors, ASACs, and SACs to go even if it is against their wishes. While I would never want to work at OPR, if the person in charge was similar to the above-described SAC, at least I would believe an intelligent employee would be making major decisions. If the organization handpicked more shining stars to serve at OPR, maybe it would be less, less... well, less f——d up is the only way I can put it.

SOLUTIONS TO THE OPR DEBACLE

For OPR to have even the smallest particle of credibility with FBI employees, one of two things must occur: It must be abolished and the investigations left to an outside agency (I do not advocate this), or in the alternative, OPR must be radically revamped. Both inside and outside the bureau, there have periodically been calls to completely eliminate OPR and leave internal investigations of misconduct to an outside agency similar to the inspector general's office. I do not advocate this radical step because the investigators of the misconduct must have, at minimum, a passable knowledge of how the entity that is the FBI actually functions. For this simple reason, OPR personnel must be current (or, at a minimum, former) FBI special agents. Agents understand how investigations take place, and they realize the periodic ethical quandaries employees will face. OPR should continue to be run by the FBI, but its operation and employee selection must be completely altered.

OPR Should Not Address or Resolve Minor Administrative Misconduct and Mistakes

Currently in the FBI, management often uses OPR as a bailout. Instead of handling minor errors in judgment or mistakes directly, bureau management immediately notifies OPR at HQ, and all decisions are removed from their hands. Management is often unwilling to make minor inquiries to determine if any serious misconduct took place, and instead, an electronic communication is immediately fired off to HQ, stating the earliest of early facts, and OPR invariably opens an investigation. This initial step is a waste until inquiries reveal a serious ethical lapse. Some initial inquiries should be made before any decision is made to refer the matter back to OPR. Often, management is afraid to make any inquiries because they feel they will be second-guessed by OPR if it is determined that a serious ethical or criminal lapse occurred. This is ridiculous because a field office manager could quickly conduct a few interviews and determine the likely validity of minor issues. The FBI selects top-level SACs to make equitable decisions regarding employees. Administrative misconduct should be no different. If it is important, refer it to OPR. If it is minor, scold and discipline the employee as well as his boss. Simple as that!

To explain this recommendation more succinctly, the employee's direct superiors should handle all administrative mistakes, and OPR should not be involved. The superior should be able to recommend a sanction (perhaps this could be appealed to one level above the supervisor), and then the decision is final. In this way, ridiculous inquiries will not be sloughed off to OPR. OPR investigations should be reserved only for serious misconduct or illegal activity by employees.

OPRs Should Never Be Handled in the Field

A separate cadre of trained investigators (supervisors and above) should be set up at HQ to handle all OPRs. This would ensure consistency in investigation and punishment. Secondarily, a supervisor will not have to investigate an employee he or she routinely interacts with. I am not saying it is impossible to be impartial, but it might be difficult if there is a history (good or bad) between the employees. It makes sense that a separate group of competent investigators handles the serious OPRs. Remember, because of suggestion one, they will no longer be burdened with petty and minor administrative mistake OPRs.

A group of trained investigators handling OPRs will add credibility and experience to the process. As OPR investigators handled more cases, they would become increasingly familiar with techniques and skills needed to complete a thorough OPR case. These skills are divergent from what a routine manager now does on a daily basis. If investigators are skilled at OPR investigations, they should be encouraged to remain there, and since going to OPR will not be elective, we can select competent employees for the position.

I would like to provide a personal example of why having trained investigators familiar with completing OPRs is essential. I was being investigated by supervisors in my office concerning allegations of off-duty misconduct. One of the two supervisors was very competent, and one, a complete loser. Two superiors must be present during any interview of a subordinate. While there was no question my misconduct occurred and while I readily admitted it, the incompetent supervisor repeatedly tried to trap me into incorrect statements. After the signed sworn statement was in its initial form, I made numerous corrections to eliminate inaccuracies. The errors had obviously been added by the less competent supervisor to more quickly resolve the matter. It all worked out (for OPR) in the end, and they leveled the maximum possible punishment on me, undeservedly. But that is how OPR works. I am only an agent anyway.

The importance of the above story is that they sent in one complete buffoon to be part of the interview. If OPR were set up correctly, two well-trained and experienced investigators would have been sent from headquarters. I cannot say that the final decision would have been any different, but at least I would have been certain it was investigated competently and without bias.

Judgment of Guilt Should Be by a Jury of Your Peers

It is a well-accepted legal doctrine that in criminal cases, innocence or guilt is judged by a jury of one's peers. In other countries like Iran, a judge renders the final decision. Yet I do not live in Iran or Pakistan. My radical solution for OPR decisions is fairly simple. After all the facts have been argued and OPR makes a decision, that decision should be appealable to a jury of the accused's peers. Obviously, this would be available only for serious issues, probably those involving unpaid suspensions for thirty days or more up to dismissal. If an SAC was accused, three SAC equivalents would be randomly selected to hear the arguments of the accused as well as OPR, and they (SACs and OPR) would render a decision of guilt and punishment. If it was an agent accused, three agents would be selected, and so on. Judgment by a jury of your peers—it sounds very American, does it not?

Each OPR Case Should Be Judged on Its Own Merits

Toss out the presumption of guilt, consider all factors, go through the processes, and when all is said and done, let each case rest on its own merits. This is what we do in the United States; we never presume guilt. Let the facts stand on their own.

CONCLUSION

Any changes to OPR would be positive. All employees know that there must be a final arbiter for misconduct, but how the FBI handles it now is a joke. OPR, as it exists today, is like a cancer that destroys essential organs. I feel OPR is akin to the melanoma I have. It started as a mole on my skin, where, if removed correctly, it would have been of little consequence. Unfortunately, it was not removed correctly (doctors make mistakes too) and subsequently moved to my brain. From there, all manners of procedures were tried to eliminate it from my body. As to success, the jury is still out (pardon the analogy). What I must do now is everything possible to ensure it does not metastasize again and destroy my entire self. OPR is like my melanoma: If you cut a piece of it out, that may not be enough. It must be eradicated entirely from the FBI in every form in which it now exists.

As a final coda to this chapter, I must admit that despite all my logical criticisms of OPR, it is unlikely it will be eliminated even in noncriminal administrative matters. Therefore, if anyone reading this is an FBI employee under the scrutiny of OPR, take heart and fight tooth and nail. It is just like cancer. The harder you fight, the longer you will live, even if you do eventually die. Imagine yourself as the mouse in the cartoon about to be eaten by the cat. The mouse's last act of defiance is to give the flying middle finger to the cat—think like that mouse if OPR is trying to get you.

I have a wonderful friend who, after a misdeed, was transferred to an office she did not want to work in. Everyone expected her to be a difficult, malcontent problem, but she became a close friend and often my investigative partner. While she had a chip on her shoulder, she worked hard and was respected by everyone. She completed outstanding cases and was respected wherever she went. The lesson in this story is you can prove yourself better than OPR by not letting the bastards keep you down. It is just like cancer—if you keep upbeat, you are much more likely to prove a fatal diagnosis wrong.

In the handbook *Cancer as a Turning Point* by Lawrence LeShan, PhD, the author discusses how a positive attitude and a strong belief that one is a special and unique self can stimulate the immune system to fight cancer. He refers to a case study of a woman who loved ballet. She never worked in the industry but had toiled long hours in the garment business to put her family through school. The woman in LeShan's case study was uneducated but decided, after being diagnosed with terminal cancer, to write a history of the New York Ballet. The project, though initially frowned upon by her family, became a focus and helped her through a very dark time. The same was true for me when OPR wrongly punished me and nearly destroyed my faith in the FBI. Instead of allowing OPR to destroy me, I refocused.

During my thirty-day punishment, I remained positive and began writing my first book. The success of that book convinced me to write a second book, which would critique but, in the long run, assist the FBI. I always had tried to help the FBI be successful through my efforts within the organization. When I realized I could write successfully, it gave me renewed energy to write this second book and be a continued positive force within the FBI. Hopefully, I will become healthier, just as I know the FBI can. A complete revamping and redefinition of OPR can only help the cause. Agents are sworn to protect and defend the Constitution and constitutional rights. Therefore, agents must also be afforded the same due process rights when they are the subjects of an OPR inquiry. This should be an absolute guarantee.

CHAPTER 4

EEO, Racism, and Sexual Bias

Equal employment opportunity (EEO), racism, and sexual bias are correctly perceived as important issues within the FBI. All organizations in today's society, both governmental and private, must strive to ensure that no discrimination occurs within their operation, and detailed laws and formal regulations are designed to address these problems. While these laws and regulations can be burdensome, and often cumbersome, their intent is appropriate and laudable.

The problem in the FBI is not the regulations but the way the bureau opts to address underlying causes and effects. In plain and simple terms, the FBI is scared. The organization fears an appearance of disparate treatment on the three issues of equal employment, race, and gender. Yet the FBI has relatively few deficiencies in the area of discrimination. As with any sizable organization, the FBI has its share of bigots, sexists, and homophobics, but deep-seated problems exist infrequently.

The FBI makes a discernible effort to foster cultural awareness of minority groups via promoting African American, Native American, Hispanic, and numerous additional festivities within both the bureau and the community. Many of these cultural days also involve great food and cultural displays, which are well attended by office employees. While FBI people are not always paragons of culture, everyone loves a good meal.

Most everyone in the FBI relishes the diversity of cultures our employees possess. While the bureau is not as culturally diverse as America itself, efforts are actively encouraged in that regard. The true difficulty concerning bias and ethnicity is that it only takes a few bad apples to ruin a good apple pie. The FBI must actively ensure the bad apples get their just deserts but let us not burn down the entire bakery in the process. As I have noted before with cancer in the brain, you do not send the patient to a guillotine for a final remedy.

The FBI treats every EEO allegation seriously, and it should. However, if initial investigation seems to confirm that the accused was innocent and has no pattern of prior incidents, we must cut some slack. Conversely, if there seems to be a pattern of cultural insensitivity, the employee should be expeditiously fired. Unfortunately, today in the FBI, the EEO office tends to investigate fully the most frivolous claims and subsequently recommend ridiculous sanctions, including attending sensitivity classes. Come on now! I do not expect law enforcement to be replete with talking boxes of sensitivity. Cops and agents deal with, arrest, and interact with criminal and terrorist scum. A bit of an edge is warranted, effective, and needed.

As an example, we do not need to address most complaints of foul language in the squad room or office. I myself have a foul mouth. I had it as a kid, and ten-plus years undercover in the drug arena was unlikely to correct it. To file an EEO complaint about my potty mouth serves zero function. Sometime back, I worked with an agent who happened to be a Mormon. We got along great, but I noticed she cringed every time I let loose with some f-bombs. I asked her if it bothered her, and she answered that she did not particularly like it but it came with a law enforcement job. After that, I made a conscious effort to watch my language—more watching my language than if she had made a formal complaint. By the way, after a couple of years, I overheard a few "g-damns" out of her too. Law enforcement will do that to anyone.

The basic idea here is that coworkers, and management, can more effectively deal with little issues than EEO investigations can. Similar to OPR, let the organization address big EEO and discrimination issues and leave the small stuff to routine management channels. In no way do I diminish legitimate EEO complaints. These should be dealt with harshly and quickly, but do not confuse two drastically different scenarios. The FBI handles (and legitimizes) far too many frivolous complaints. A few years back, I received a copy of an FBIHQ office of EEO affairs memorandum, addressing the percentage of EEO complaints filed in government versus the private sector. I would die to have saved a copy of that memo (though perhaps, with my type of cancer, "die" is the wrong terminology). Anyway, this piece of trash written by EEO complimented government employees for filing a higher percentage of such complaints, indicating it showed government employees felt free (and safe) from retribution. The findings also claimed to demonstrate greater honesty on the part of government types. Bullshit! (Oops, sorry to my former Mormon partner.) The numbers actually showed one of three things:

1. Government types file more frivolous EEO complaints.
2. Government employees commit more EEO violations.
3. Private sector employees are afraid to file complaints.

In my experience, the first or second explanation is correct because private sector employees have the same legal EEO whistle-blower protection government employees possess. I believe the definitive and most likely answer is that government employees file more frivolous EEO claims.

What are the true EEO, racism, and sexual bias issues in the FBI? Hold on to your hats, sombreros, berets, yarmulkes, etc., and lighten up too.

> Prejudice is not held against people
> because they have evil qualities,
> evil qualities are imputed to people
> because prejudice is held against them.
> —Marshall Wingfield

THE FBI EMPLOYEES ARE ENCOURAGED TO REPORT "STUPID CONDUCT" AS EEO RELATED EVEN WHEN IT IS NOT

I honestly do not know how to detail and more cogently explain the above heading. FBI employees are bombarded repeatedly with admonishments against discrimination, sexism, and homophobia. Each employee sees the memoranda regarding these issues, and each employee is commanded to never lower himself or herself to discriminative behavior and to immediately report such instances. Almost every employee agrees with and realizes this inherently; no one wants to operate in a hostile and discriminative environment. Yet somehow, the bureau screws up even this simple directive. The overemphasis on monitoring employee conduct leads to repeated EEO complaints that do not involve legitimate EEO issues.

FBI employees realize that if they allege discrimination in hiring, promotion, or environment, the world is put on hold. Accordingly, bad, incompetent, or malcontent employees realize an EEO complaint will immediately stall and delay legitimate administrative employment sanctions.

If the FBI wants to admonish you, claim some manner of bias, and the process is soon halted or at least slowed. I was involved in investigating an OPR on a support employee. The allegations are irrelevant, but his response (once he consulted an attorney) was that the investigation was racially motivated. Even the mention of this immediately forestalled a quick resolution of the matter. The investigation clearly demonstrated inappropriate activity unrelated to the employee's race. Yet his race began to determine how the matter would be addressed.

In the above example, the employee was convinced that because of his race, he was immune from adhering to the standards each employee must follow. Similarly, when an employee does not secure a promotion, minority groups are encouraged to question the decision and determine if it was based on the employee's minority status. This is an unfortunate fact in the FBI.

When one is diagnosed with cancer, the doctors stringently question the patient concerning heredity, genealogy, and background. My doctors advised it was more than likely related to the Scandinavian side of my family tree. Cancer was indiscriminate in choosing me as a host for its growth. Should I be able to complain that it was racially motivated? Of course not! Most often, when bad or unfortunate things happen, it is simply factual reality. Was I unlucky? Perhaps, but that is not the issue. The world, and the powers that be, did not discriminate against me. You must play the hand you are dealt in the best way you can. You can fight the rare instances of actual discrimination by showing you are a better and more competent employee. If I have to fight my genetics in my battle against cancer, I will do that as well.

Most times, discriminators point to a perceived weakness. Often, there is not an actual weakness. Yet even if there is a weakness, such as when you have a genetically predisposed cancer, you do not give in: you must try harder. Perceptions and opinions are like your teeth and gums. If you keep them clean and disease-free, you will be healthier and have better breath. In a similar vein, do not believe every bad decision is discrimination related, but strive to remove every truly proven "cancerous" (read "racist, sexist, and biased") employee. As my mom always said, "Brush your teeth."

> The gem cannot be polished without friction,
> nor man perfected without trials.
> —*Chinese Proverb*

As in society, biases and prejudices are prevalent in the FBI.

I will offer my opinion succinctly in one sentence (in a second), and I will try to justify it in a few brief paragraphs. Yet I emphasize here (as I have stated elsewhere) the opinions in this book are solely my own. Other agents might feel differently, but I believe many, if spoken to off the record (or off the polygraph), would agree.

Okay, okay, here is my sentence (as a friend of mine might say, "Oh boy!").

Other than in very rare instances of individual bigots, the FBI currently does not discriminate against African Americans or Hispanics, though it routinely discriminates against white males, homosexuals, and in particular, females.

Before I continue, I should do my mea culpa here. I am a white male. I am Protestant, though Catholic trained, and a practicing Zen Buddhist. A detail of my visage and background would more clearly identify me as a dark-skinned, ruddy-toned, whitish type, yet I still contracted melanoma, dang it! I provide my basic type to disclose any inherent "stuff" I may have affecting my subsequent verbiage. I prefer to think of myself as neutral, and I could provide you, as my readers, a detailed list of my friends, girlfriends, bosses, coworkers, and family as a reference, but I prefer to briefly summarize as follows:

Family – Nothing but a wonderful, loving, and stabilizing mix. Thanks!

Co-Workers – My finest agent partner was a female wunderkind, who, even when she relocated to San Francisco, never knew how good an agent she was.

- The best supervisor I ever saw was a Hispanic-surnamed agent who relocated to Miami and took the management world by storm. However, I am convinced that my Spanish language skills remain superior to his, courtesy of my drug tours in South America.
- The best agent I ever saw, bar none, was an African American man who could do it all and who remains in San Diego as a supervisor. If I could personally choose a new FBI director, I would select Mr. D.

Bosses – Please give me all the same SACs: I have never had a poor one. Regarding supervisors, ASACs, and above, give me the minorities and females who fought the good fight, and the organization will do well.

Girlfriends – It is none of your business who they were. I hope they are all happy.

Friends – They are all identified, each one, under the previous categories.

Okay, now you know about me. What about the FBI? In the FBI, homosexuals are routinely treated poorly, and this is particularly so with male homosexuals. Still, law enforcement is replete with gays and, particularly, lesbians. Originally, the bureau, during background investigations of applicants, asked sexual-orientation questions. The organization justified this by believing homosexuality was an issue an agent could be blackmailed with. If criminals (or more importantly, foreign governments) determined that an agent was homosexual, he might disclose secrets to remain in the closet. While today's FBI has an official stance that homosexuality is not an issue, routine discrimination against gays is common. For this reason, homosexuals rarely come out once hired by the organization.

Females routinely face discrimination and sexual harassment in today's FBI. I would go so far as to say that the discrimination against females might be systemic even in the new millennium. Men and women are clearly different and distinct beings. There was a bestseller entitled *Men Are from Mars and Women Are from Venus* for a reason, but discrimination does not need to be the aftermath of these differences. Women bring a unique, insightful, and decidedly different perspective to the work of law enforcement and counterterrorism. Women can be just as tough as men when needed, but most female law enforcement members do not feel any particular need to kick ass unless it is necessary. This decided lack of machismo often makes females superior interviewers, planners, and innovators over their male counterparts. The majority of male FBI agents relish the occasions when females are present on the squads because it is one more resource and knowledge base that can be drawn upon. The FBI could indeed benefit from more female employees. While the FBI continues to treat women employees disparately and some active discrimination does exist, better education can remedy this. Continued emphasis on educating employees concerning sexism in the workplace can accelerate the progress being made. I honestly believe that with continued effort, sexism in the FBI can be eliminated.

No one would be more qualified to discuss bias against females than a longtime female agent would, and I asked such a person to comment on the issue. She is of the opinion that bias and discrimination have diminished noticeably in the twenty or so years she has been an agent. Additionally, she agreed that a small percentage of female employees magnify problems because they are aware that wrongly claiming discrimination will make things easier for them. Finally, and perhaps most significantly, she had observed that sometimes when females made mistakes, it was treated by management and coworkers as a much-bigger deal than if the gaffe had been made by a male employee.

While sexism and homophobia are issues in the FBI, prejudice against African Americans and Hispanics does not exist. In fact, African Americans and Hispanics are promoted and treated better than white counterparts. While periodic and singular instances of racism exist, they are isolated and insignificant. My time in the organization has absolutely demonstrated to me that African Americans and Hispanics are promoted (and treated better) disproportionately to their competence. This clearly displays the fear the organization has concerning frivolous lawsuits, which may be filed by employees who are African American or Hispanic. Within the last ten years, two major class action suits were filed against the FBI by African American and Hispanic groups. While both suits were groundless, the FBI rolled over and ceded to both. The most egregious example was the BADGE, or Black Agents Don't Get Equality action.

While the scope of this book is too brief to fully address the BADGE suit, suffice it to say that the majority of employees (black and white) believed the allegations were divisive to the organization and largely unfounded. The evidence in the BADGE suit showed there was limited or no discriminative impact against African American employees. Black Agents Don't Get Equality, beyond being embarrassing grammar, was a legal farce. Most of the statistics delineated that there was no disparate impact and that there were a higher percentage of minority managers than in the general agent population. More minorities received disproportionately favorable treatment when clawing up the management ladder, receiving a higher percentage of promotion because they were African American. I always believed a better acronym for the lawsuit might have been BADGER: Black Agents Do Get Equality—Repeatedly. This acronym would emphasize how the lawsuit badgered the FBI into capitulating in a case where no major violations were ever demonstrated.

SOLUTIONS TO EEO, RACISM, AND BIAS ISSUES

Extensive Training of Employees Should Take Place Concerning Homosexuals in the Workplace

Concerning education, I do not mean standard sensitivity-style training. The FBI is not the military, and a "don't ask, don't tell" mentality is inappropriate. Sexual orientation is solely a personal decision and not a business decision.

Your preferences at home should never affect your job situation. My suggestion is that the manner of education should be developed by outside groups, homosexual employees, and EEO officials in the FBI. Simple as that!

Employees should be confronted with the extensive documentation that females in law enforcement are equal and just as competent as male counterparts.

Again, in this area, education and personal interaction will demonstrate to employees that the different skills females possess are an advantage in law enforcement. Numerous studies have identified females as having superior interpersonal skills (particularly with other females), and these abilities often make female interviewers more effective. Good management is often in a position to identify situations where a female agent serving as the interviewer will immediately lead to incriminatory statements by the witness.

I should also emphasize here that most females do not have the physical strength or body conformation to single-handedly disable a three-hundred-pound subject in a hand-to-hand confrontation. Realistically, however, male agents are rarely asked to do that either, and many of the FBI's male agents would not know how to handle a physical confrontation. I fear many might run for the exit. The FBI can train female employees in the use of martial arts and personal weapons (hands, feet, knees, etc.); overall, everybody has room for improvement.

Finally, concerning females, the FBI must acknowledge that there are situations where a male agent might be more suitable or, conversely, a female. You would not send a female to conduct surveillance in a nude-dancing cabaret, nor would you ideally want a male agent to strip-search a female suspect. In similar ways, African Americans, Hispanics, Asians, and other minority groups may be best suited for certain assignments. Many of these assignment selections are routinely based on legitimate consideration of sex, race, or ethnicity.

The definitive conclusion here is that with appropriate education of employees, our diversity can be our greatest strength and not a divisive weakness.

There Must Be a Screening Process to Determine If an EEO Complaint May Be Bogus

Employees in the FBI know that if they play the race card and claim a decision was racially motivated, the world stops turning on its axis. The same is true with sexism and ethnicity complaints. A process must be expeditiously developed to determine if the initial complaint has legitimate merit. If the screening process (which would be conducted by bureau management) found it highly unlikely that a violation occurred, the matter should be stopped immediately. If some evidence tends to confirm an actual violation, then go forward with a full-scale EEO investigation.

I intended here to provide a real-life example of a very frivolous EEO complaint filed in my current office by a female employee. I decided, however, that this would be inappropriate because although the complaint was ridiculous, the people involved would be embarrassed if I rehashed the saga. Instead, I decided to relate a different example that I believe shows how all of us (FBI or not) take everything much too seriously.

A female agent friend of mine complained that it was getting to the point where men would not compliment her on an attractive outfit. When there is fear that someone will file an EEO complaint when a man says, "Nice dress," we have allowed EEO to destabilize the organization. I believe I was raised in a culture of gentlemanly behavior that understood it is appropriate to offer a compliment when it is deserved. During my discussion with my friend, I advised that the distinction between compliments and sexism or harassment is usually quite apparent:

Compliment: You have nice legs.

Sexism: You have nice legs, and they would look great over my shoulders.

In addition, while my female agent friend agreed, she did note that many ladies might (if stated in the correct context) also consider the second remark a compliment. The story above comes back to common sense and knowing your audience. If there is a possibility that anything you say might offend, do not say it. Nevertheless, have a sense of humor and a little fun out there too.

To Eliminate Frivolous EEO Complaints, the Bureau Must Punish False Accusers

A major obstacle to successfully addressing EEO problems is that far too many ridiculous racial, gender, and orientation complaints go forward. If an initial screening process cannot slow the growth of frivolous and fraudulent EEO complaints, measures that are more drastic must be considered. A radical idea that would greatly limit irrelevant, malicious, and fraudulent complaints is to eliminate whistle-blower protection if a baseless complaint is pushed forward.

If initial inquiries disclosed that the complaint was frivolous, the complaining individual would be advised of that finding. If the complainant chose to continue the issue and the subsequent full investigation revealed no merit to the initial complaint, the complainant would be administratively sanctioned. The logic to this is inescapable. If racism or other discrimination is alleged, this is a serious charge and is not something that should be dismissed lightly. However, it is just as disruptive to concoct a false charge and continue to allege it in the face of logical rationality.

Let me provide a few examples of stupid complaints that our current EEO system allowed to go full course. As you review these examples, consider whether after resolution, the complaining party should have been sanctioned for false allegations and causing disruption to the organization.

An employee alleged he was discriminated against because he was not a native Spanish speaker. This occurred because while he spoke Spanish, he was not born in a Spanish-speaking country. He alleged the discrimination occurred when he was not offered the same quality of cases native Spanish speakers received. What the heck does that mean, and is there even any relevance? The issue boiled down to one person who spoke excellent Spanish (the native speaker) and one who was not as fluent because he learned it later in life. I wish my own Spanish was better too, but the above situation is not discrimination. Unless there were other reasons, such as being overworked, why would any manager select a less-qualified employee? While this is patently clear, the FBI continued to push forward and investigate the frivolous issue.

While women are discriminated against in the FBI, some females exacerbate the problem by filing silly and disruptive EEO complaints. A former female agent explained that in her former field office, women were frequently applying for jobs for which they were not qualified. When they did not get the position, they claimed discrimination based on gender. My experience is that females are discriminated against more frequently. Still, when females make false claims, there must be a means to punish them for false allegations.

CONCLUSION

Equal employment opportunity, racism, and bias issues in the FBI can be more effectively addressed than the organization does currently. After a full and complete investigation, exact specific sanctions on those who commit EEO-related violations. Additionally, sanction all those who file ill-intentioned, fraudulent, or incorrect allegations. Just as in cancer treatment, incorrect diagnosis and suppositions can cause more emotional harm than a correct diagnosis does. If a doctor advises a patient that the cancerous site is inoperable, this levels a great weight on a patient's shoulders. If more complete diagnostic tests disclose the cancer might be operable (this is what occurred in my case), the patient will be confused. Was the first doctor a poor doctor? Did one of the doctors lie or mislead? I believe the reaction I had to an incorrect operative diagnosis was similar to what an employee falsely accused of an EEO violation feels. They feel betrayed and desire to have the false accuser punished or sanctioned. The above cancer situation was one of the few occasions where I felt some true animosity toward my doctors. While I know the error was not malicious, it hurt. In the FBI, we must strive to limit false EEOs (by the promise of sanctions), and if the cancer of an EEO violation is actually there, we must battle it actively and aggressively.

Finally, being the victim of prejudice is a horrendous and unfair burden for any employee to shoulder. Prejudice in the FBI must be eliminated. I am certain I have been the victim of prejudices during my life, but I never experienced them as pointedly as when stricken with cancer. While most everyone (both inside and outside the FBI) was supportive, I did notice I was sometimes perceived as damaged goods. There were periodic hints that I would not be competent or able to work.

As I author these paragraphs, I understand it is likely I will never be as fully functional as before. It has been determined that after all the treatments and medication, I am no longer able to act as an FBI agent. I sought medical retirement and left the organization. I would never allow my condition to be a detriment to the FBI's important mission. Yet that decision should be my own, in correct consultation with FBI officials. I should also not suffer discrimination based on a misperception that a person with cancer is automatically incapable of contributing to society. We can all play nicely together in the sandbox that is the FBI, can't we?

CHAPTER 5

A Zen Interlude
What Does Cancer "Feel" Like?

The purpose of this chapter is a brief respite from the drone of my previous text describing an equivalency between the bureau's shortcomings and cancer. To understand this chapter, you must watch (or remember) the film *The Shining*. After watching this movie, based on the Stephen King novel and starring Jack Nicholson, realize what Nicholson's character is experiencing is similar to having cancer. The experience of cancer is much greater than the physical pain involved. The emotional toll is much higher. A cancer patient is lost, confused, angry, and depressed. What Nicholson's character endures is much like cancer and cancer treatment: delusions, irrational expectations, family unit disintegration, and pain. Finally, the last scene in the movie where the title character is lost in a disorienting frozen maze can be seen as akin to either working in the FBI or suffering from cancer!

The feeling (directly from Stephen King) is as follows:

> "All work and no play makes Jack a dull boy. All work and no play makes Jack a dull boy. All work and no play makes Jack a dull boy. All work and no play makes Jack a dull boy. All work and no play makes Jack a dull boy. All work and no play makes Jack a dull boy. All work and no play makes Jack a dull boy. All work and no play makes Jack a dull boy. All work and no play makes Jack a dull boy. All work and no play makes Jack a dull boy. All

work and no play makes Jack a dull boy. All work and no play makes Jack a dull boy. All work and no play makes Jack a dull boy. All work and no play makes Jack a dull boy. All work and no play makes Jack a dull boy. All work and no play makes Jack a dull boy. All work and no play makes Jack a dull boy. All work and no play makes Jack a dull boy. All work and no play makes Jack a dull boy. All work and no play makes Jack a dull boy. All work and no play makes Jack a dull boy. All work and no play makes Jack a dull boy. All work and no play makes Jack a dull boy. All work and no play makes Jack a dull boy. All work and no play makes Jack a dull boy. All work and no play makes Jack a dull boy. All work and no play makes Jack a dull boy. All work and no play makes Jack a dull boy. All work and no play makes Jack a dull boy. All work and no play makes Jack a dull boy."

CHAPTER 6

Today's "Me Generation" Employee

Many newly hired agents are afraid to take extensive risks because they are worried they will get in trouble; instead, many just show up to collect a paycheck. The potential value and importance of a job as an FBI agent make it essential to minimize slackers and selfishly motivated employees. The bureau is charged with a great responsibility concerning criminal activity, foreign counterintelligence, and terrorism. It is unconscionable when personal selfishness on the part of an individual employee detracts from the FBI's mission.

Many newer agents tend to be so afraid of making a mistake and being punished that they never put forth the diligent effort required. Some are so afraid of the stick that they never attempt to grab the carrot. I believe the analogy is similar to someone with cancer who never explores more nontraditional concepts like clinical trials. Clinical trials are treatments that are considered somewhat experimental because, as of yet, there have been limited participants in the studies. Still, here is where risk-taking can provide the greatest advantages. Many treatments sound outlandish at first blush yet are immensely successful, and significant research on animals occurs before human trials are considered. Still, while it is decidedly linked to medical theory, there is significant risk involved. Someone had to be the first patient to be irradiated or subjected to high-dose chemotherapy. While these are accepted treatments today, I take my hat off to the first patient who said, "What the hell, inject me with a chemical cocktail." It takes some moxie and spinal fortitude to undergo cancer treatment. FBI employees could learn to be similarly aggressive and risk oriented. Additionally, every risk-oriented mistake (if committed in honest conscience) can teach other employees how to avoid similar errors. In cancer treatment, even if clinical trials (or other treatments) are unsuccessful, the information gleaned may assist subsequent patients.

Be aggressive fighting cancer battles, and likewise, fight hard (even uphill) in the FBI. Never give in to complacency; the FBI job is far too important to cave in to petty personal desires or others' selfish wishes.

> To give real service
> you must add something
> which cannot be bought or
> measured with money,
> and that is sincerity and integrity.
> —Donald A. Adams

The adage that "there is no 'I' in 'team'" is indicative of what a bureau employee should believe. The FBI exists solely to serve the American public to the best of each employee's personal abilities. Unfortunately, far too many current employees believe the organization is only alive to guarantee them a paycheck. While there is no "I" in "team," there clearly is in *FBI*. Many (perhaps a majority) of personnel act in their own interests to obtain administrative promotions but forget why they entered the FBI originally: to serve. This is identical to cancer physicians overly concerned with salary: they forget that their purpose is to heal. There was no comparison, however, between the percentages of my cancer doctors who were extremely dedicated versus dedicated FBI agents. My physicians were almost universally brilliant, hardworking, and kind. The only doctor I largely disliked was a Dr. Dumopolous (name changed to protect the guilty), who told me I was on my deathbed long before I had a chance to fight or was due under the sod.

Doctors and agents are here to serve the American public, and that is their only duty. Salary and perks are irrelevant. As an FBI agent (or a doctor), if you ever feel a moment of selfishness, recall why you came to the job initially. It will not be for the money. If you are beginning to feel self-important in your position as an FBI agent or you believe serving the public is not sufficient, get out! It is about the American citizen, not any single employee.

The major issues concerning the FBI's selfish employees are as follows:

CURRENTLY, MANY NEWLY HIRED EMPLOYEES IN THE FBI ROUTINELY DISCOUNT AND DISREGARD SUCCESSFUL, ESTABLISHED, AND PROVEN OLD-SCHOOL TECHNIQUES

Many in the newest cadre of FBI employees believe only the newest skills and techniques are valuable. Many believe the vast majority of our mission is singularly linked to counterterrorism. This command is directly from upper management (and particularly Director Mueller himself), yet putting all the eggs in one basket will clearly de-emphasize extremely important non-counterterrorism issues.

I bring up the overemphasis here to provide an example of the organization making a snap judgment and failing to heed old-school ways. The history of the FBI (see appendix 1) easily demonstrates the success achieved by utilizing historically proven techniques, including undercover operations, wiretaps, informants, etc.

To begin to be so self-centered and believe that there are only new ways that are most effective is the height of arrogance.

While each employee must be innovative, history is always the best teacher. One of the paths the FBI has mistakenly followed recently is to position newly hired employees in jobs that are immediately critical and demand deep-seated experience. Every employee should want to be challenged to the utmost of his or her ability, but virtually no one walks into the agent position ready to take charge of a major investigation. If more senior and competent employees assist in the training and guidance of newer hires, fewer mistakes will occur. In the old bureau, no one ran or managed a major section of an investigation until he or she had at a minimum three to five years in the FBI. We need to return to understanding the value of such experience.

One of the single greatest ideas in FBI history was the concept of the diversified hiring category. This category allowed the FBI to hire college graduates (with a minimum of three years' work experience) from any occupation. This might include former military personnel, former law enforcements, or former ballet dancers. This category brought energy, vibrancy, and innovative thought to the agent position. Most importantly, it was a program that gave the FBI the option to hire employees who possessed real-world law enforcement experience. The FBI still hires qualified language specialists, accountants, lawyers, and computer geeks, but there at least was a means for the organization to hire some normal nontechnical types. I acknowledge inherently that the FBI needs technical specialists and techno-whiz kids, but we need law enforcement experience most of all.

The category recently has been downscaled significantly. It is selfish and foolish for the organization to believe it no longer requires a significant former military and law enforcement entourage. Who will make the arrests if we have no one with previous arrest experience? Arresting and dealing with criminals and terrorists is not a skill you pick up on a street corner! Bottom line: no cops equals no experience.

At a recent party, a group of young agents was watching the television show *Cops*. During one of the arrest scenes, a new agent commented that he found the show disturbing due to its violent nature. What the f——? We are out here dealing with some very violent folks. While I find *Cops* a little cheesy, I am surely not disturbed about it. The reason I am not disturbed is that I have been fortunate enough to make hundreds of street arrests and learned from each and every one. Learn from every arrest because it might save your life or, more importantly, someone else's life. This younger agent's attitude demonstrates a lack of comprehension and ignorant egotism and selfishness. Open yourself up cognitively and learn the very best available techniques. One of the greatest old-school arrest lessons I ever learned was to always consider every agent's opinion before an arrest or major operation. While anyone may have a great idea, most often, it is the experienced agents who will present the most cogent concepts. Even today, experience counts for a great deal in the FBI, and it is not all about logging on to computers, data loading, and "clean situations." Listen to the senior agents; they have a vast wealth of knowledge and experience.

IN THE FBI, AS WITH MANY GOVERNMENTAL ORGANIZATIONS, EMPLOYEES ARE NEITHER PERSISTENT NOR DILIGENT IN THE FACE OF A MASSIVE BUREAUCRATIC MORASS

Often times in law enforcement, and particularly in the FBI, it seems that disappointing news occurs after bad news, ensues after terrible news, and follows horrendous news. As an agent, you are working your rear end off, but the organization itself is placing roadblocks at every turn. Your logical and somewhat important case is disapproved, and your supervisor would not be able to identify a terrorist or a criminal with a sniper-scope. The bureaucratic mess is an indelible black mark on the FBI. I hope that the book you are now holding will contribute to general public education of the bureau's deficiencies that can be minimized by public and internal input. The absolute key for the individual employee is to keep trying harder. Find a way around the bureaucratic stupidity and be innovative. As an FBI employee, you must be diligent, but you do not have to drudge. Do not merely go into the office and show your face (as many worthless current agents do today). Each employee must try harder, especially in the face of difficulty; no whining is allowed. Trust me absolutely, as someone who has a virulent form of cancer and has undergone uncomfortable and unpleasant cancer treatments that your sorry ass is damn fortunate to be toiling in the FBI trenches. While you are an FBI employee, appreciate what you have. FBI employees (and particularly agents) have unique opportunities to help society combat crime, espionage, and terrorism. We are fortunate to have an opportunity to assist America.

I made a concerted effort to remain a full-time working special agent, but in 2004, my doctors advised me that, to recover fully, I would need to seek permanent disability. The doctors also advised me that working even part-time might lead to a complete relapse, and possible death. I was absolutely devastated. While I have numerous criticisms of my organization, I revered the work and most of my coworkers. I was forced to start full-time sick leave before my disability, and I felt extremely lost and unhappy for many months. Still, I had to keep proceeding forward. My decision was based on my doctor's advice to try to get well and educate myself about metastatic melanoma cancer. I, with the assistance of my wonderful girlfriend, Kathy, conducted extensive research on viable treatment options from surgery to chemotherapy to experimental treatments. I promised to always keep trying and putting forth effort in the direct face of hardship, just as all FBI agents must do in periods of investigative difficulty. Even after I suffered a series of unexpected grand mal seizures six months after my first round of surgery, I did not give up. I was depressed, but I vowed to fight on, hoping I could get healthier and continue to be a positive contributing factor in my family's and friends' lives. I also made a firm decision to always be there for the FBI if I was ever in a position to continue to provide further assistance. I ensured that all my work was current and all cases and informants were appropriately passed on with sufficient explanation to other qualified case agents. I made every effort to ensure that my being forced to leave the FBI would not disturb the mission of the organization. I believe it was my duty to do that much for the American public, and to do any less would have been cowardly. I left because it was the correct decision for my family personally, and it provided my family the greatest likelihood I would survive and be able to continue to provide for them financially. Besides, on a selfish note, if you read my first book *Zen and the Successful Horseplayer*, you know I want to make it so I can continue to attend the Del Mar horse racing meeting each year.

NEW AGENTS BELIEVE WHAT THEY LEARNED AT THE TRAINING ACADEMY AT QUANTICO IS SOMEHOW CONNECTED TO THE ACTUAL JOB OF BEING AN AGENT

Within the last few years, the training at Quantico has been completely refocused to emphasize the new FBI priority of counterterrorism. I am of the opinion that no newly hired employee should be led to believe that what he or she learns at Quantico, Virginia, is in any way related to the job that the agent will perform on the streets. As I write this chapter, one of the most brilliant and stand-up men I ever dealt with is one of the chiefs of Quantico. This individual, who was a former new agent classmate (long ago and far away), is one of the most spectacular agents I have ever interacted with. Still, the FBI was able to co-opt and corrupt this outstanding individual into the "terrorism party line." The essential issue here is that now everyone who goes through Quantico is narrowed in focus rather than broadened. Specific skill can always be taught on the street after graduation, whether it be in the criminal or counterterrorism arena. Virtually nothing learned today at Quantico translates into what an agent actually does.

It is essential that great agents be in all positions and not merely terrorism jobs. When the organization overemphasizes terrorism, it is being selfish and missing the broader concept; it also does a great disservice to potentially valuable employees. For a period during the analysis of what cancer treatment I should undergo, some of the doctors advocated an immunotherapy stimulation infusion (using hamster ovary cells, of all things). It potentially seemed like a good option, and I fully researched it and considered it. When my initial blood tests disclosed my white blood count was too low to be considered for the trial, I felt as though I had been cut from the varsity basketball team. I was devastated, but when subsequent tests determined I was eligible for the trial, I ran the full gamut of emotions from relief to blistering anger. Doctors must understand that people are investing emotional energy trying to obtain treatment, which may or may not have some potential for success. Blithely dashing patients' hopes on the rocks incorrectly is unconscionable. To eliminate someone from a study because they are "too sick" needs to be explained as a possibility up front. Additionally, specific alternatives should be offered for treatment. This is also true with FBI agents. Not all FBI employees are good at all things, and newer agents in particular need to broaden their skills as often as possible. All potential options should be provided instead of force fitting everyone into international terrorism. It is unreasonable to believe all employees will be good at counterterrorism. Instead, place them where they are most useful to the organization. Advising every new employee that terrorism is the only primary road will lead to a great degradation in overall FBI skill level. This is like forcing everyone into the same cancer study even though separate studies have a higher potential for success. Currently indicating to all employees that the entire FBI world is almost singularly about terrorism is creating many unhappy employees, and relatively few senior agents aspire to be terrorism types. Is it necessary that all focus should be on terrorism? No, this selfishness comes from upper management down and is quickly instilled in new agents.

If the opinions of experienced senior employees were more frequently considered and less emphasis was put on newly hired employees, the FBI would function more effectively. This methodology would allow newer employees to see the organization in a more correct historical context. This context must specifically include that it is not the training academy that offers the most value. It is what you will learn in the field. We must actively educate and cross-train all our people. When agents are trained in only certain areas, there is an immediate assumption on their part that these are the only areas the FBI considers valuable. However, the most valued agents are often criminal experts who understand how the federal legal system operates. They are also the most competent to handle coordinating arrests. In this subsection, I am in no way suggesting that pure terrorism and foreign counterintelligence agents are not great employees, but we require as broad based an employee as is available. Training at Quantico should be related to all tasks agents are likely to perform. I admit that I am somewhat biased in that I believe dealing with intelligence information is more rudimentary than interacting with real, living human being bad guys, yet, in truth, my personal opinion here is unimportant. The true issue is that agents must be able to complete both types of tasks efficiently and effectively. Quantico needs to revamp its focus by training agents in all the tasks they will be asked to complete from criminal to antiterrorism. Further, a program should be initiated where new agents are sent to the field and rotated through various squads for a series of months so they understand what agents actually do on other squads. This rotation period should take at least twelve months and encompass six squads. The FBI currently has a ludicrous system in which a new agent is stationed at FBIHQ for one to two months after Quantico and before the agent's first field assignment. There, they answer telephones concerning investigation questions from various field offices. This is absolutely inane. What the hell could they know? They have never even worked an active investigation. These TDY (temporary duty) HQ employees are also each paid TDY money (read "your tax dollars") amounting up to approximately $10,000 for this "effort." Instead, after their initial training at Quantico, these new agents should be sent directly to the field where they would receive practical on-the-job, apprentice-style training with experienced agents in various disciplines from criminal to terrorism to cyber crime.

THE FBI CREATES A CULTURE OF SELFISH EMPLOYEES BY ALMOST AUTOMATICALLY CATERING TO SELF-CENTERED DEMANDS

The FBI frequently (and sometimes almost inadvertently) indulges its self-centered employees more than silent hard workers. The FBI is a large organization, and it is difficult to oversee. This oversight is frequently complicated by malingering workers who understand that if they complain of a mistake originating elsewhere, they are unlikely to be punished. Even during the penultimate FBI investigation of the 9/11 incidents, investigating the New York City (World Trade Center), Pentagon, and Flight 93 (Pennsylvania) terrorist attacks, a few FBI workers in Phoenix complained they were being asked to work long hours and overtime for which they did not receive compensation. September 11 was the single most important terrorist incident in world history. Each FBI employee should have been honored to have the opportunity to work 24/7 on this attack. Be assured that most FBI personnel did work seven days per week and obtained little sleep, yet a significant number of employees embarrassingly put in their normal hours and complained they would work no additional time without mandatory overtime pay.

I worked something akin to forty-five days straight after 9/11, trying to help in any way. I had during my drug career authored a dozen or so Title IIIs (court-authorized wiretaps). So I spoke to the Phoenix agent handling the investigation and asked if there had been consideration given to seeking monitoring authority of particular individuals' telephones in the Phoenix region. The case agent responded that the squad wanted to listen to the telephone but did not have sufficient people to write the affidavit. He explained that it would require a foreign interception surveillance authorization (FISA), which was different from a Title III. I offered to help write the rough draft FISA and cobbled together a horrendous first draft, which the case agent reviewed and corrected and submitted to headquarters for approval.

I was actually proud that I had been able to provide some help (no matter how meager or half-assed) in a terrorism venue. I had not assisted much, but I had helped some and learned a lot working with an experienced terrorism agent. Ah, but let no good deed go unpunished! Unbeknownst to me (I was too busy working), a group of people on the terrorism squad (I was still on the drug squad at the time) complained they should have written the FISA because it might lead to promotions. When the case agent and supervisor later told me this, I actually believed they were speaking in jest. No, the actual complaints had been made to management. No actions ever came down over this, but I was demoralized to see the depths into which the FBI could sink. Why would anyone be looking for credit? You might put in some tiny piece of the puzzle and help humanity. To the Phoenix office's credit, they did not give much quarter to the allegations, but the incident demonstrates some of the mentality in today's bureau. I advocate here that when employees whine in this manner, they should be dressed down immediately and given even more work.

> Life is a short day,
> but it is a working day.
> Activity may lead to evil,
> but inactivity cannot lead to good.
> —Hannah Moore

During the two-month period around 9/11, I worked almost every day and took time off only to grab a quick workout at the office gym, eat, or sleep. Most employees did the same thing, but a significant portion worked their normal hours and nothing additional. Approximately a month and a half after the 9/11 incident, I went into the office for a few hours and then decided to go play a quick round of golf. I rarely tell strangers my occupation, but on that golf outing that day, I spoke up. The other three in the foursome thanked the FBI for its efforts and added that they felt honored to meet someone helping to protect the country. Two of the three younger businesspersons even inquired how to apply to be an agent and asked if I could help them get in. I was humbled. Here were citizens of my country thanking me for the FBI's help. I returned to work the next day with an increased fervor to do more. FBI employees must realize that our citizens trust and rely on us.

The harder FBI employees work, the less time they will have to whine. I believe invalid complaints and whining should be punished by management just as quickly as actual laziness and sloth. Even when there is a true reason to complain, such as when you get cancer, don't bother. If you are too busy fighting cancer and educating yourself about the disease, you will never be a bad example to others. You will additionally have a greater likelihood of success.

SOLUTIONS TO COMBAT THE SELFISH "ME" EMPLOYEES

No Initial Temporary-Duty Assignments to FBIHQ

The current policy of sending new agents from Quantico to HQ for thirty to sixty days as a learning experience needs to be immediately eliminated. This malformed policy puts inexperienced people at HQ, potentially providing an opinion on a field office question, and it makes the TDY people believe they should even have an opinion. A new agent probably should not consider his thoughts rational until he has been in his first field office at least six months. This useless and expensive one month at HQ could much more effectively be utilized in the agents' first field office, training with senior employees.

The FBI Should Mandate Agent Rotational Transfers

When I first entered the FBI, agents spent approximately two years in a smaller office (e.g., Sacramento, California) and then transferred to a large office (e.g., Los Angeles). After that, when eligible (ten to twenty years on average), you could request transfer to an office that had an opening, regardless of its size. The current system (which is being revamped) allows many new agents to stay in one field office far too long. While relocation can be tough on a family, it brings the employees closer to the organization and establishes esprit de corps. Additionally, it broadens agents' experience by allowing them to observe how divergent offices conduct investigations. The gains clearly outweigh the family hardships during transfers. I strongly endorse this idea of Director Mueller's and hope he will activate and enforce the rotational transfer concept. Additionally, eliminating the current policy of new agents spending thirty to sixty days at HQ wasting TDY (temporary duty) monies can offset some of the cost.

All New Employees Transferred to the Field Should Be Trained and Assisted by Experienced Senior Employees

Regardless of how clever and good a new agent is, he or she should work in an apprentice capacity under experienced personnel before being assigned investigative duties. The FBI pays lip service now to the above concept but does not actualize it. Often due to labor shortage, new employees are independently conducting investigative work too soon; new employees should not be assigned to proactive investigations. Instead, the bureau should adopt an apprentice-style program similar to the training medical specialists receive.

One of my principal oncologists was tremendously overworked. I would go in for appointments, and you could see the sleep deprivation effects in her eyes. She subsequently hired an associate doctor to assist her with some aspects of her work. The newer doctor learned from the more senior doctor and was able to conduct some of the routine procedures. This worked to both doctors' advantages. The more senior one obtained support and assistance to free up time, and the newer apprentice received valuable experience and on-the-job training. The other benefit to working with a senior doctor (or agent) is that the new hire observes that no one has all the answers. Senior employees frequently consult with others to get an even more informed third opinion. Finally, working with senior employees should diminish arrogance in new hires because they will observe that this is an inappropriate way to comport oneself (either as doctor or agent).

Cross-Train and Educate Employees in Many Areas of FBI Discipline

Obviously, not everything each individual employee does has equal value. Currently, the director is mandating that terrorism is "numero uno." This mandate came directly from the president of the United States, and the director is following orders. However, this does not mean that the FBI should de-emphasize divergent skills. While all FBI employees (and doctors) gravitate to a specific specialty based on interest, skill, and needs of the organization, talent should be based initially on broad-based experience. Doctors in medical school do not spend their first years learning about lymphatic carcinoma (cancer in the lymph nodes). Instead, they learn about bones, tissue, internal organs, and diseases in general. After this initiation, they receive instruction about specific areas of interest like cancer or heart disease.

How doctors are instructed is exactly how the FBI should cross-train its agents. Teach everyone the generalities of arrest, terrorist ideology, criminal and aberrant behavior, etc. After this, slowly allow the employee to garner a specific discipline or expertise. Doctors act this methodology out over five years of medical school and another three to five years of training in a specific area. Believe me when I state that FBI agents are not stupid, but we are generally not in the same brain-wave arena as physicians. If it takes doctors that long (including apprenticeship) to perfect their trade, the FBI could stand to keep newer agents under a more extended apprenticeship and learning program as well. The longer an agent stays in an apprenticeship-style role, the longer he can be instructed in cross disciplines.

Eliminate the "Where Is My Car?" Mentality

FBI agents leaving Quantico should be advised that they will someday be endowed with great powers and commensurate responsibility. They should also be told this would be unlikely to occur in the short term. New agents are now told that it is quite likely they will be actively involved in major cases and be responsible for major matters. This does a twofold disservice to the new employee: it induces false expectations, and it fails to tell the employee what to actually expect.

When I graduated from Quantico over twenty-five years ago, we were told to go out and listen to the senior agents, work hard at whatever job you were assigned, keep your mouth shut, and learn. I believe I generally heeded that advice and became a competent agent. Today, agents are emerging from training with actual full-blown opinions and even arrogance. A few years back, I was the acting supervisor of my squad while the boss was temporarily in another position. On a Wednesday, an agent leaving the FBI Academy, ultimately destined for my squad, phoned the squad secretary and stated he would be getting to Phoenix on Thursday night and that his first day of work would be the following Monday. He mentioned that he would like to "swing by" the office and pick up his official government car on Thursday so he had it with him to drive in Monday. The young man, who is actually a fine FBI agent who received some bad advice from his Quantico class counselor, is fortunate I was not there to answer his call. I would have instructed him to take a cab from his plane to the office the moment he touched down, put on a suit, and meet me in the office immediately. Why the hell does he even think he is getting a car anyway? When I came in the FBI, you drove your personal car to and from the office for a year or two.

In today's kinder and gentler bureau, we usually do provide transportation from day one, but new agents should be instructed to expect nothing and offer everything. The concept needs to be drilled into the training unit at Quantico that these young men and women are lucky to be agents and that, in time, they will have more than enough duties and responsibilities and will eventually be given a car (usually a nice one these days).

CONCLUSION

The basic and most obvious way to stop selfishness is for the organization to stop hiring and supporting self-centered employees. Everyone wants to be successful and find his or her job rewarding, but cockiness and egotistical arrogance are hardly building blocks of an organization created to serve citizens. Egotism also stifles successful interaction with state and local law enforcement.

When I returned from Saudi Arabia after my brain cancer diagnosis, surgery, and radiation therapy, I was virtually a driveling idiot, dragging my legs and speaking in a slur. One of the things I had to do virtually immediately was pay my government credit card bill for travel expenses I incurred during my trip. I could not have written it if my life depended on it. My girlfriend and an agent friend put the entire report together for me, based on my incoherent writings and ramblings, and the supervisors made sure it was approved. This is when cancer victims feel support. I actually cried trying to explain my voucher costs to my girlfriend—I was that incoherent. Yet what that agent friend (and many others) did to help me while I was suffering the worst mental effects of the surgery proved to me that there is enough care and competence in the FBI to prove all naysayers wrong. I received great support from my SAC, Charlene Thornton, who allowed me to work from home when I was not allowed to drive. Additionally, I received a much-appreciated call from my former SAC, Guadalupe Gonzalez, who spoke to me for almost an hour, encouraging me and indicating I was a valued FBI employee. When I personally observe that style of dedication and concern among FBI employees, I am certain the bureau can right itself. In the same way, cancer victims want their doctors to listen to their issues, questions, and concerns. No one going through cancer understands their own difficulties better than the patient does: the patient has the greatest insight into his or her pain, discomfort, and related issues. Doctors must listen and be supportive of their patients. But most of all, they must listen. Similarly, the FBI must listen to its own citizens.

Seek out the very best for the FBI and when selecting doctors. Listen to the best-trained and most senior personnel. When I had a mole removed from my chest more than ten years ago, the doctor (who was not a cancer specialist) said it was likely no problem. The mole ended up being a melanoma mole, but then the doctor felt he "got it all." He suggested only periodic checkups and follow-up (no recommendation for irradiation, additional resection, or lymph node removal was advocated). Another agent associate had the same thing occur (melanoma mole diagnosis), and the doctors took out lymph nodes, insisted on physicals every six months, etc. He has never had a recurrence and is completely healthy today. The mistake I made in my first situation is I only went to a dermatologist for a mole, and had I gone to a knowledgeable oncologist for a follow-up, I perhaps would never have suffered the metastases from my chest. Always seek out the best. In the FBI, when you need an expert in terrorism, locate the senior terrorism brain surgeon, and you will be less likely to have terrorists metastasize. "Me generation" employees need to learn that the FBI has qualified experts on virtually all law enforcement subjects. Draw out and extract that wisdom and experience. In this way, perhaps in twenty or twenty-five years, you will be a gold mine of experience for subsequent newbie agents. The progression across generations is what can make an organization like the FBI both fluid and strong. Listen to the past, keep your eyes open for the future, and never be selfish.

Finally, there are numerous psychological steps people with cancer can take to help stimulate their systems to battle the disease. Doctors advocated a positive frame of mind. People who are positive, motivated, and diligent are much more likely to succeed in their battles against cancer. I add that people who are motivated, aggressive fighters are also likely to be the best FBI employees. Find your raison d'être (reason to be) in the organization, and strive and struggle. If you find the answer, you will come to see your value is not in what you have accomplished but in what you can now do. Work hard and never be selfish, and you will do well.

CHAPTER 7

Avoid a Deadweight FBI Doom

The FBI has some of the hardest-working employees in either private or public sector operations. Unfortunately, the organization also employs a significant number of lazy, low-energy slugabeds. There are people in between these polar opposites, but the real-life dichotomy is quite dramatic. I would estimate that within the agent portion of the FBI population, 20 percent of the agents complete 80 percent of the work. Even more dramatic than the 20:80 ratio is my personal belief that approximately 5 percent of agents do no work whatsoever! It is quite possible that the 5 percent figure is actually even higher. This is a dramatic breakdown, where laws changing retirement, dismissal policy, and hiring policy must be implemented and imposed on the FBI by legal mandate. This is an area where public pressure on legislatures and the FBI can only create positive results. The FBI itself will never initiate the necessary changes. Additionally, many changes will necessitate more work, oversight, and accountability on the part of management. It will not be easy to streamline a behemoth like the bureau, but it is integral to creating a more successful operation.

Now is the moment in time to make administrative movements become more efficient and effective. During the revamping related to the emphasis on overseas operations, counterterrorism, and HQ's management of individual investigative matters, FBI employees are expecting change. While I do not agree with the singular emphasis on terrorism, mine is only one employee's opinion. Regardless, if since 9/11 our hidebound agency has been able to take baby steps toward morphing from a primarily criminal to a dual terrorism/

criminal organization, we have demonstrated some flexibility. It is flexibility that I believe many of the individual employees of the bureau possess.

FBI employees are very different from what they are portrayed on television and in the movies. We are not all beauty queens and gorgeous bodybuilders with high IQs, nor are we routinely arrogant assholes who do not work well with local law enforcement. Most agents are fairly smart, enjoy working with the locals, and usually are not so physically heinous that they cannot get a date on New Year's Eve. Our employee deficiencies are relatively infrequently linked to a lack of competence, and it is more often in the diligence area where we fall short. It is difficult to train someone to be smarter, more intuitive, or smoother. Yet what can be done immediately is to induce all employees to work more efficiently and harder. Even less competent employees can produce more if placed in positions where only extreme diligence is required. Every employee knows ways he or she can work harder and more effectively, and each must make this occur even in the face of other employees' obstructionist inertia.

> It is better to lay your life
> upon the Altar of Worthy Endeavor,
> than to Luxuriate and perish as a Weed.
> —Albert L. Williams

What the FBI must actively strive to accomplish is to limit and punish laziness and commensurately encourage and reward concerted effort. The principal deadweight issues are summarized as follows.

DURING THE APPLICANT-HIRING PROCESS, THE FBI FAILS TO ADEQUATELY SCREEN AGAINST HIRING SLOTHFUL EMPLOYEES

The FBI currently conducts a background criminal check, psychological tests, and interviews of applicants for the agent position. While the process is well intentioned, it does not go far enough. Many people entering the agent ranks are excellent bull-shitters but cannot back up the bullshit with facts. My close friend was on an applicant interview panel and asked the applicant to provide an example of a moment when he or she resolved an ethical dilemma. Agents come across ethical issues every day, and this is an outstanding applicant question. The candidate (not surprisingly, an attorney) immediately responded that he had something happen that very morning. While at the FBI office, he had purchased a newspaper, and the newspaper boy had incorrectly given him change for a $10 bill rather than the $5 he had given the boy. The applicant explained he had immediately remedied this mistake by returning the five bucks to the kid. As my friend told me the story, my immediate reaction was, in law enforcement, we have more serious ethical conundrums (e.g., do we shoot this person, do we seek to obtain that individual's cooperation, or do we drop this case, etc.?). It was a weak example offered by the candidate, but not too big a deal. No great shakes until my friend continued the story, saying he had not believed Smarmy Boy's answer. My friend went downstairs and found the only paperboy on duty that day. The young paperboy said he did recall the applicant (after a description), not because he had mischarged him $5, but because the kid said he was going upstairs to be hired by the FBI and was extremely cocky. Guess what? Due to some diligence by one agent, we will now avoid Mr. Smug being hired by the bureau. Unfortunately, due to previous lawsuits, our new applicant-testing procedures do not allow for follow-up questions unless they are specifically included in the testing protocol. Independent questioning outside scripted questions allows the interviewers to probe weak or inconsistent answers. We must allow applicant interviewers to follow up on weak or inconsistent answers.

Lazy people can come with great résumés and good glad-handing skills. The applicant process must pierce through these veils. This issue is particularly applicable when we hire former military officers. Some of the best agents are former military, but so too are some of our most lazy. Particularly, former military are sometimes the pinnacle of getting by on "Yes, sir" and "No, ma'am" without any substance. To combat this in the interview process is relatively simple. Ask for detailed specifics of what the applicant (not his entire squadron) accomplished during sample time periods. Also, specifically explore any disciplinary action taken against the former military officer.

The step, which will wash out lazy former military, is simple. Have current FBI employees (who were formerly in that particular military service) check back on Lieutenant Smith, and ask what the real deal was. This should be an automatic process, and it would ensure the FBI minimizes our percentage of bogus former military. About nonmilitary applicants concerning laziness, all references and a series of business associates should be queried on the specific issue of sloth. Even a hint of laziness should be examined dutifully by the interviewers, and if confirmed, the applicant should be rejected.

It is essential to minimize deadweight employees because they damage the organization on multiple levels. First and foremost, they fail to do the necessary amount of work. Second, but perhaps more importantly, they destroy some of the morale of the efficient hard workers. It is somewhat analogous to cancer. A healthy, highly efficient human machine is inflicted with cancer in one area (for example, an aggressive and usually fatal cancer such as pancreatic cancer), and this healthy being can become critically ill and die very quickly and painfully. This fits the FBI employee who enters the organization with a good résumé but, once inside, quickly learns how the system works and begins to immediately watch the nap channel after each lunch. This "sleeping disease" is not acquired once in the FBI; it existed in the new employee before his or her hiring. We need to ensure these employees are extricated prior to being admitted through the entrance to Quantico. This technique of identifying and rejecting the stealth sloth before hiring would be a plus for the FBI.

Sometimes, however, this is not possible, and the slugs will be identified only after being hired. Here is where the deadweight employee acts like a slow-acting cancer, which slowly but surely destroys the organization, cell by cell, body part by body part. In these situations, the employee gradually does less and less work once hired. He or she learns how to fool the system by putting paper in the files but never really completing substantive work. This is an issue that management should act on more effectively. Once a sloth employee has been empowered and passed through Quantico with badge and credentials in hand, it becomes more complicated and difficult to cut out or treat the slow-acting but not immediately fatal cancerous employee. Again, however, I stress that while this is curable once inside the organization, the best course of action is to prescreen potential employees for sloth and reject them before they are hired. Cut out cancer at the earliest opportunity. In most cancer treatment, if it will not significantly harm the organism, surgical removal of the tumor is the preferred first option. In the same way, cut out cancerous employees ASAP—do not hire them in the first place or, if hired, eliminate as soon thereafter as feasible.

THE FBI DOES NOT MONITOR CLOSELY ENOUGH THE TIME THAT EMPLOYEES SPEND ON ANCILLARY DUTIES

In the FBI, many agents (and some non-agent personnel) have jobs that they complete, which are designed to be secondary to their primary investigative functions. These "outside interest" folks also participate in SWAT, firearm instruction, defensive tactics coordination, seized-computer-hard-drive inspection, evidence response, and numerous other important functions. I begin this critique by avowing there are many who are involved in these types of ancillary functions that are some of the FBI's best and brightest. They are completing these additional duties in addition to their normal investigative responsibilities. However, some people in these programs utilize these duties as an excuse to perform their primary work less effectively. The FBI must diligently monitor the specific time employees engage in these activities and determine if there is even the slightest perception it may be interfering with traditional casework.

As an example, many employees are able to be on SWAT or ERT and be a full-time agent. This is an ideal situation because everyone is attempting these ancillary jobs because they are each individually interested in that type of work. Everyone is then functioning successfully, and an agent should be encouraged to enroll in these positions because these are important jobs that contribute significantly. However, we must ensure that our principal focus never shifts away from putting bad guys in jail via complex investigative methodology. The agent position can remain multifaceted and interesting even while the primary work of "criminals directly to jail" continues as primary emphasis.

THE FBI'S CURRENT EDUCATIONAL AND INSTRUCTIONAL PROGRAMS FOR ON-BOARD EMPLOYEES ARE MUCH TOO NARROW

Currently, most instruction of new agents is conducted during multiple training sessions at Quantico, Virginia. After an employee is sent to the field, training is then received periodically in a field office or the employee revisits Quantico for refreshers. I have no problem with this, but I would strongly advocate greater emphasis on a third and fourth leg for this instructional chair. Chairs are not usually made to stand on three legs, as I recall my geometry, because there is greater stability on four. FBI employees should repeatedly receive training from outside agencies on that agency's new investigative methods. We should obtain training on how the CIA operates, how the DEA handles drug cases, and how the local police departments operate. We can learn just as many new innovative skills from them as they can learn from us. The FBI may not incorporate all these techniques, but we can learn from each one, and the instruction will make the FBI more rounded and informed about what is being done on the street. This type of instruction could significantly broaden an agent's perception.

My fourth leg to the chair would simply be to have new agents assigned a senior employee as a training agent when they arrive in their field office. This process is actually in place now but is followed only minimally because we are understaffed. Well, that is unfortunate, but this is one of the areas where the senior employees will have to tough it out for the good of the organization. Senior agents should expect to continually work more and harder throughout their career. A senior employee conducting ongoing training of more junior employees is just one additional task that should be expected.

> Service is the rent
> that we pay for our room on earth.
> —Lord Halifax

If you are a new agent, work harder to make up for your lack of experience. If you are a senior employee, work harder because now, with your knowledge, you have more to contribute. Every senior employee should be willing to mentor not just one but several employees for as long as needed.

PUNISHMENT AND SANCTIONS FOR LAZINESS AND POOR PERFORMANCE ARE NOT HANDLED EFFICIENTLY OR QUICKLY

The lag time between when an employee performs poorly and when he is sanctioned is forever, or at least semi-eternal. Sanctions for lack of effort must be swift and painful. These sanctions should involve cuts in pay, demotion, and written reprimands. Currently, the FBI plays much too nice with its bad and malcontent employees because of the fear of lawsuits. The organization must buckle down and fight poor performance with increased sanctions. For example, supervisors would be authorized to impose an immediate ninety-day cut in pay until the employee's performance improved. Even awful agents tend to be cheap, and a smack in the pocketbook might get them on track (or at least improve the agent's performance).

THE FBI SETS ITS STANDARDS FOR EMPLOYEES MUCH TOO LOW, AND THE CURRENT PASS/FAIL EMPLOYEE RATING SYSTEM IS NOT JUSTIFIABLE

When the bar is set too low, everyone can walk over it. The requirements to become an FBI agent should be very stringent. These standards must include intelligence, experience, and physical conditioning; we should strive for excellence, but instead we shoot for mediocrity and often do not even hit that mark. Recently, the physical conditioning standards at Quantico have been lowered. You do not need to run as fast, as far, or possess as much physical strength for push-ups and pull-ups. This was changed because the FBI lost a series of lawsuits filed by employees, saying these qualifications were not job related. Here is an example of where a weak FBI rolled over. All law enforcement departments have physical training (PT) standards. The FBI should be raising its bars, not lowering or removing them. The current standards are not too challenging, but they set a minimum level of physical condition. The reason these standards were established is so all employees understand that there are certain physical requirements that are demanded from all. Physical standards are justified because no one should ever be injured or die because his partner was so physically out of shape that they could not assist during an arrest or other situation. We cannot continue to allow people to make it through Quantico without passing PT or firearms because it creates a culture in the FBI where it is acceptable to fail. The bureau's mission is too important to allow a mind-set of failure to creep into the organizational consciousness and become acceptable. If you fail at Quantico, you should be immediately dismissed, and if you subsequently win a lawsuit, then the FBI should pay you an agent's salary for cleaning the floors and lockers in the office gym. Never give in to mediocrity.

In cancer treatments, the individuals who are healthy before being afflicted with cancer are the ones most likely to survive and recover. I was very healthy before stricken with brain cancer. I ran a mile or two every day, lifted weights five days a week, and I ate health smart. Being physically fit did not stop me from getting cancer, but my doctors said it probably saved my life during the brain surgery and seizures. People who are physically fit and high in energy are more likely to have success in their war against cancer. In much the same way, FBI employees who are highly motivated and driven compete better in the wars against crime and terrorism. The FBI needs fighters and those who have overcome adversity. This is identical to cancer patients: fight and you have a chance, give up and you have none. Though Western film star John Wayne eventually died of cancer, he held it at bay for many years. He made a movie (*The Shootist*) about a gunslinger who struggles with terminal cancer even as he continues to win the shootouts. I think about that John Wayne character often and hope there is some of him inside me. Cancer might have eventually killed Wayne, but this cultural icon told cancer to "get the hell outta here" three times, and the first two times, the cancer listened and ran away. This is what I am attempting to tell my own cancer—"Go away." If all I get is two more years, good enough. Yet whatever time I have, I will relish it and do the most with my time. So when you throw the sod on me, make damn sure I am dead, because if I have a reason, I just might reach through the dirt. There are still some important things I want to do to help this world, this country, and my organization. If we keep lowering our standards, a culture of mediocrity will be created where no one knows how to fight any longer. Fight harder and you might just win a lot of your battles and wars. Set standards high and then find ways to achieve them; never give up.

Pass/fail standards are now sometimes utilized in the FBI to rate employees. While all grading standards are sometimes capricious, to knuckle under and only provide pass/fail ratings is inexcusable. Rate employees, challenge them to improve, and analyze the results on a sliding scale. Any rating system is better than just saying you passed. The FBI should want and demand the top one-percenters. On the opposite side of the equation, the Hells Angels Motorcycle Club (HAMC) members are called the one-percenters because they are supposed to be the meanest and most vicious 1 percent of all society. If the HAMC can aspire to that, we should be able to have the FBI aspire to hire the top 1 percent of people interested in law enforcement. J. Edgar Hoover would tell you the FBI hired those types when he was around.

THE FBI QUITE FREQUENTLY DOES NOT LISTEN TO ITS OWN BOSSES (UNITED STATES CITIZENS)

The FBI is a quasi-political organization, and the president of the United States appoints the directors for ten-year terms. Liberal Democratic presidents often name more liberal directors. Conservative Republicans name more conservative directors. The director's job is "somewhat" immune from political machinations. Agents' jobs are to enforce the laws under the jurisdiction that we are given. The FBI has authority to enforce laws ranging from covert funding of terrorism to the Switchblade Knife Act. Clearly, the issue for the FBI is how we should prioritize which laws to enforce. I do not believe many citizens give a damn if someone has a switchblade, but they care a great deal if al-Qaeda is setting up a covert operation in Albany, New York.

Prioritization of investigative activity and resources is the linchpin to FBI success or failure. This prioritization must come from the American public after thoughtful interaction with knowledgeable FBI employees. The FBI should not be what we tell the people we are. Instead, the bureau should make every effort to become what the public wants us to become. These public recommendations will be very fluid and variable across time. The historical appendix to this book demonstrates how our greatest successes have come when the FBI is malleable and responsive to historical upheavals, changing its focus from draft dodgers, to spies, to wise guys, and so on. Much of this refocusing was based on the organization understanding historical context had changed and that there were now different, more primary dangers.

The president is now mandating that the FBI's principal focus be counterterrorism and related problems. My concern is whether the FBI appropriately queried our citizenry to determine if we should be vacating areas such as violent crime, fugitives, and white-collar crime to devote almost our entire resources into a single arena. This has never occurred in the approximately one-hundred-year history of the organization. Is it appropriate to go this way now? A majority of current employees would say this route is a road to ruin. Still, it is irrelevant what we want. What matters is what you, the informed citizen, want. The FBI must immediately begin to conduct detailed public surveys across demographic and political lines to determine what crimes should be investigated and what laws should be enforced. This is one of the primary reasons I wrote this book so that readers can be provided informed advice on what the FBI should investigate. I believe that the overemphasis on counterterrorism will destroy the FBI because it will narrow us in focus so excessively that our investigative and traditional law enforcement skills will be degraded. Yet it may be possible to overcome this if it is what the public demands.

My informal contact with citizenry still profoundly indicates that you want the FBI to continue to investigate and arrest many other types of violators (fugitives, computer-fraud perpetrators, white-collar criminals, etc.). Many citizens I have spoken with want these areas emphasized more than counterterrorism because a bank robber, a serial rapist, or a drug dealer is significantly more likely to personally affect their lives. All want terrorism investigated, but when the actual risk is explained, many citizens want (and expect) the premier law enforcement agency in the world to be more than an internal CIA. My informal poll is only that—informal and not statistically verifiable. An official tasking to speak to the populace on this issue should be conducted immediately. We work for you. You tell us what you want us to do! This point is very important because there is a strong divergence of opinion within the FBI. Many employees working to combat terrorism argue correctly that no citizen wants another 9/11 to occur. But no one wants his or her daughter or son to be kidnapped or sexually assaulted. The answer the FBI often responds with is that it can do all these things if the American public provides the bureau with increased funding. Nevertheless, we must prioritize: taxpayers cannot afford unlimited funding.

WAYS TO MINIMIZE DEADWEIGHT AND EMPLOYEE LETHARGY

Conduct Reverse Citizens' Academies to Learn What Citizens Actually Want the FBI To Do

Here is a radical but extraordinarily simple solution to eliminate deadweight while determining exactly what our public wants—ask them. One of the reasons the FBI appears slow to respond is that we often fail to advise the public exactly what we are trying to do. The public believes we are hunting down terrorist operatives in Cleveland, Ohio, when in fact we are completing most of our investigation in Kabul, Afghanistan. It may be that if we explained the necessity to be in Kabul, the public would agree, but perhaps not. Maybe you want us here in the United States protecting you from organized street gangs. To determine what you want, we should utilize a vehicle we already have in place—the Citizens' Academy.

Currently, in most major field offices, every six months or so, the FBI brings in twenty to thirty typical citizens and explains to them what the FBI does. I would recommend turning this concept on its ear. Bring these people in (after a brief background check to protect security) and explain what the FBI is capable of doing and then ask them what they would most prefer the FBI investigate. This is identical to the manner in which an employee of any company would ask their boss what tasks need to be completed this month, this year, and in the next ten years. Tabulate and analyze these ideas countrywide and develop time-pertinent plans to address these issues.

Encourage Open, Outside-the-Box Thinking and Allow Unique Personalities to Flourish Bureau-Wide

Universally, lazy employees (in any company) are paragons of boredom (if there is such a thing). Not everyone lacking a personality is a bad worker; some people are merely a trifle staid. However, what I have observed in the

FBI is that many of our employees who are perceived as eccentric are the best and most outstanding. Jim Morrison's quote "People are strange when you're a stranger" immediately jumps to mind. When an agent looks at something from a nontraditional angle, he or she may discern a way to break open a case no one else even considered. Outside-the-box agents are the employees who went undercover into Haight-Ashbury in San Francisco in the 1960s, who decided to develop a union leader/mobster as a source, and who indicted the controller of the largest financial institution in Arizona.

Investigators who do things nontraditionally tend to be looked down upon by our agency's more buttoned-down types. The "that agent is strange" types are scrutinized by management until they clearly demonstrate extraordinary competence. Quite often, they possess extensive talent by the very virtue of their unique perspectives. In my own case, while not the sharpest pencil in the box, I always tried to view an investigative problem nontraditionally. My experience of fifteen years of undercover work offered me unique ways of interacting with criminals. It also proved invaluable when faced with stumbling blocks. It takes extra effort to take nontraditional routes to an indictment in the federal system, but when it works, an agent has proven truly valuable in his job. It does present risks to the employee attempting a new technique, but as in cancer research, if we do not try new things, we will never learn. Someone has to be first, and then an entire series of people have to confirm the validity of the technique.

I met with my primary oncologist and was advised that, after speaking to my entire team of doctors, I would be given a chemotherapy regime of temozolomide and thalidomide. The doctors warned me that while they all believed that this was the best protocol for me based on the progression of the disease, health, and other factors, it was still not a proven treatment. The doctors explained that while the treatment appeared to be effective in thousands of individual cases, the combination still had not reached the three thousand validations needed before the medical community could officially embrace it. For once, my doctors sounded like FBI headquarters management because unless you can show hundreds of occasions where a type of investigative technique worked, we probably will not authorize its use.

Allow Agents to Get in Trouble

As an FBI agent, if you are periodically being summoned (or even routinely) to upper management's office for making a mistake or getting in trouble, you are probably doing a good job. The saying "Let no good deed go unpunished" is legendary in the bureau. Agents frequently put entire investigations together where dozens or even hundreds of subjects go to jail, but a minor miscue in some aspect of the case results in disciplinary action against the agent. Talented and driven agents stopped worrying about this a long while ago. If you join up with the FBI and you expect to be successful, expect your knuckles to be hit with a ruler frequently.

Lose the Losers

The FBI is tremendously burdened with deadweight do-nothings in its most senior agent ranks. Agents understand that after fifteen to twenty years, no matter how little they do, no sanctions will occur. This matter must be remedied by legislative change and public support. Everyone who enters the FBI agent ranks believes they will receive steady periodic pay increases and be able to work until age fifty-seven. This is a concept that must be eliminated. Clearly, there should be standards of likely pay increases based on time in, but these need not be guaranteed or set in stone. More integral, however, is that the FBI must eliminate the rule that you can work until you are fifty-seven regardless of performance. Many employees should not leave at the earliest moment (generally age fifty) either. Some very senior employees, fifty and above, continue to have the drive, skill, and motivation to be outstanding employees. I personally vowed never to become a senior agent resting on my laurels. But while I cannot impose that opinion on all others, with appropriate legislation, the FBI itself can.

There are two means to make this take hold. The initial rule change would simply become that once you are of retirement age (fifty with a minimum of twenty years' service), we do not have to keep you. If your work performance was insufficient, here is your gold watch, thanks for playing, and do not let the door hit you on the ass on your way out! If this single rule could be imposed on the FBI, our production would increase twofold. One, because senior employees would be forced to continue to maintain high-effort standards and, two, the aspect of maintaining high-effort standards in senior employees employs "the carrot." Most capable and hardworking agents receive QSIs (or quality step increases). QSIs raise employees' salaries by moving them a step up in pay, which stays with them throughout their tenure in their position. It's a positive motivator. The only difficulty is that after receiving a few of these, and/or via normal pay progression, a senior agent tops out at a grade 13, step 10 salary. Therefore, senior quality agents have only internal motivation to work extra hard because minimal or no extra money will be forthcoming. The resolution to this issue is also simple. If a senior employee is still kicking butt and taking names, reward this agent with a temporary GS 14 salary while he or she continues to do field work as an agent. This temporary pay could be limited to three years and would be an excellent long-term motivator because the pay differential would significantly increase the agent's subsequent retirement paychecks.

Motivation is much of the basis of success. In the FBI, our motivated employees produce success disproportionately to the average employee, so we must encourage effort. When one walks into a hospital (and in particular, cancer units) the doctor appears happy and enthused but looks damned exhausted. If you go into an FBI office, a whole bunch of people look too damned rested. I am not advocating sleep deprivation, but we can work a little longer and a little harder, especially during the twilight of our careers. And if bureau senior employees refuse to work more diligently on their own, force it on them.

Eliminate the Pass/Fail Rating System for FBI Employees

Until a few years ago, FBI employees were rated on a scale from unacceptable to exceptional. It was a flawed system, but at least it attempted to provide input and motivation for employees. It also encouraged competition because no one wanted to be rated below someone who was less able. Agents should not be just trying to pass. Instead, the rating system should be a motivator for them to excel.

If the FBI is defeatist and tells an employee that "it is okay, you passed," we are going backward. Successful cancer patients fight under the most adverse situations, including nausea, constipation, and pain. All the patient wants is support from the doctor that the patient is making all efforts. Even if the patient gets sicker, he is still successful, and his efforts are recognized. While this patient may not win the battle of cancer via a cure, he surely did more than pass in his efforts to go on with his life. Cancer patients cannot give up and become slackers in their fight against cancer, or they will very likely die quickly. If these people stay alive, they can continue to help in the world, and I guarantee that every survivor would feel he or she earned more than a pass on the rating scale of life.

> To preserve health is a moral and religious duty,
> for health is the basis of all social virtues.
> We can no longer be useful when not well.
> —Samuel Johnson

Conduct Random Follow-Up to Ensure Agents Do Their Job

Some of the very laziest FBI personnel complete a poor investigative effort (for example, on an interview) and then return to the office and use marvelously descriptive "bureauese," complete a write-up that seems godlike in creation. A phony write-up does not help an investigation at all. Only good, solid investigation, diligence, and some luck create success. Writing up and describing a massive dog-and-pony-show interview that contains minimal real content is worthless. This would be akin to a cancer specialist providing a patient a write-up describing his successful medical publications but not allowing the patient to review the actual publication. To avoid puffery (and downright misstatements) in FBI documents, there should be a random follow-up review of certain investigations.

A post-review squad should be developed in each field office and at HQ; they would conduct a follow-up on sample investigations. The process need not be extensive. Perhaps one out of every one hundred (or even one thousand) interviews would be reviewed to determine how effectively the original interview had been conducted and written. The actual interviewee would be re-contacted and re-questioned. The minimal extra effort would be well worth the time.

CONCLUSION

The FBI possesses some of the hardest-working, competent, and well-trained employees in the world. Still, we are burdened with an unacceptably high percentage of employees who merely skate by, cashing pretty sizeable paychecks. A senior GS 13 can earn upward of six digits per year of taxpayers' dollars. When receiving this level of pay, continuing to employ deadweight is unacceptable. We must monitor successes closely and not only allow but encourage employees to be inventive and innovative. Unconventionality is generally a potential forerunner of success on an FBI agent's part, and if nothing else, it clearly demonstrates effort.

For FBI employees to be successful, they must meet greater challenges during their careers. Incentives for performance (and disincentives for lack of effort) can induce increased effort on the part of employees. However, it is the entire institutional culture of the FBI that must change to create a spark to light a fire under the FBI's behind. I hope that some of the ideas in this chapter are a step in that direction.

CHAPTER 8

Director Mueller's "New FBI"
(AKA Star Trek the Final Frontier)

From virtually the moment (September 4, 2001) that the FBI appointed Robert S. Mueller III as director, his life as the boss has been unique. On September 11, 2001, the World Trade Center was destroyed, the Pentagon was attacked, and forty passengers and crew members were killed when hijackers overtook Flight 93. The force behind this destruction was a terrorist entity commonly referred to as al-Qaeda. These attacks immediately (and legitimately) focused virtually all of the bureau's manpower into this single investigation. Everyone working for the FBI at the time expected this, and most were willing to log whatever hours necessary to assist; this was true for terrorism and criminal agents alike. If you had a terrorism background, you had a head start, but even if you were a terrorism novice, you jumped in with both fists swinging, learned, and did what you could.

These initial months after 9/11 were a unique time in the FBI's history. Everyone was working a single identical case, though it differed in scope and intensity from region to region. Still, most every employee expected the investigation would be handled similarly in a long-term manner as every other major FBI case. We would devote full-time, massive, and intensive resources bureau-wide to the case; we would determine viable targets and solve the case. After a successful or even semi-successful resolution of the investigation, a large group of personnel would continue to complete follow-up investigation concerning 9/11. The majority of remaining FBI employees would return to their necessary duties of fighting drugs, white-collar crime, violent crime, and so on. Director Mueller, upon direct orders from President George W. Bush, remade the FBI into two counterterrorism agencies. An employee who had only been working for the FBI for slightly more than six months made the single largest snap judgment in the history of the FBI. In deference and respect for Director Mueller, he is respected bureau-wide as an intense and tireless worker who is devoted with religious-style zeal to combating terrorism. His top selected assistant was also my former SAC, who is a genuinely kind, thoughtful, and honest manager who would never consciously do harm to the FBI.

The FBI's weakness in combating terrorism is as evident to most employees as a cancer-riddled lung is visible to a doctor during diagnostic testing. The new director merely entered at a period in time when terrorist acts were perceived as the overriding concern. Had he entered two years earlier, or two years later, the organization would have been plodding along, acting in the way the FBI always had, investigating multiple violations, with various degrees of emphasis and intensity. This had always been the FBI's strength. Our wider scope of knowledge, which was broader than that of DEA, ATF, CIA, or local law enforcement, allowed us multiple investigative routes to success in various types of cases. It also provided the organization flexibility to address a particular case if no other agency had the resources to handle the matter. When Mueller changed the game, he removed the organization's flexibility, and force fit each employee into a mold. After successful cooking, the mold would be broken, and an antiterrorism body would emerge. The director couched this new ideology in new FBI priorities set forth in a bureau-wide e-mail sent out on May 20, 2002. These priorities had been spelled out long before the May 20 date, however. Mueller, to my own mind, had bailed out on his responsibility as director of the FBI. Clearly, every citizen wanted terrorism limited and 9/11 solved. Did all citizens want this attempted when the additional result would be virtually no FBI resources to combat all other criminal activity?

A close associate and friend (who works terrorism cases) dramatically disagrees with this last paragraph and says that Director Mueller did not change the game. Al-Qaeda did with their attacks. He posits further that we are the only agency in a position to battle al-Qaeda. Again, I disagree; more resources should be temporarily devoted. Terrorism is not our only enemy and probably not our most threatening.

As of February 2011, the Federal Bureau of Prison's automated information systems disclosed intriguing facts about federal inmate statistics. This data was located at *http://www.bop.gov/fact0598.html*. The total inmate population was 174,179 individuals, and while various important details can be gleaned by a close review of the information, I found the breakdown by criminal offense the most persuasive. The results showed that national security matters (which would cover most terrorism-related inmates) accounted for only ninety inmates, or less than one-tenth of 1 percent of all inmates. This seems a narrow category into which the FBI should place all its resources. While it is true that statistics are often manipulated to provide support for various divergent opinions, the actual amount of federal incarcerations due to terrorism and related activity is infinitesimal.

Based on types of offenses, Bureau of Prisons data shows incarcerations breakdown numbers as follows (percentages do not add up to one hundred due to rounding).

Drug Offenses	101,601	(50.9%)
Weapons, Explosives, Arson	30,325	(15.2%)
Immigration	23,101	(11.6%)
Robbery	8,503	(4.3%)
Burglary, Larceny, Property Offenses	6,937	(3.5%)
Extortion, Fraud, Bribery	10,169	(5.1%)
Homicide, Aggravated Assault, and Kidnapping Offenses	5,471	(2.7%)
Miscellaneous	1,871	(0.9%)
Sex Offenses	9,329	(4.7%)
Banking and Insurance Counterfeit, Embezzlement	897	(0.4%)
Courts or Corrections (e.g., Obstructing Justice)	611	(0.3%)
Continuing Criminal Enterprise	516	(0.3%)
National Security	98	(0.0%)

The mere fact that one crime is committed more frequently than others should not be the deciding factor on whether the FBI (or any other agency) investigates. Narcotics offenses are the most common criminal violations in the United States. Most honest local law enforcement narcs, DEA agents, or FBI drug agents would agree that we over enforce drug laws, but realistically, drug violations do enact an enormous cost on society. The rationale for my digression is that many citizens believe narcotics violations should be actively prosecuted. Other citizens contend that more limited antidrug law enforcement is warranted. This is another area where law enforcement must listen to its citizens. Still, if the statistics are even vaguely accurate, and less than one-tenth of 1 percent of federal inmates are tied to national security issues, should the FBI devote less than one-tenth of 1 percent of its resources to terrorism and more than 50 percent to drugs (currently there are 54 percent of inmates incarcerated for drug violations)? Of course not! This is skewing the statistics an incorrect way in the opposite direction! However, devoting the majority of FBI resources to investigating terrorism would be equally ludicrous.

Appropriate percentages of resources should be based on the number and severity of terrorist incidents and potential incidents prevented. Blithely trumpeting the war on terrorism over all other serious criminal violations does a disservice to the FBI's stated role to protect the American public. When you are an honest law-abiding citizen caught in the cross fire of a drive-by shooting in Detroit (which annually challenges Washington, DC, for murder capital of the United States), your family may want a modicum of FBI investigative assistance. Of course, the Detroit Police Department will likely be able to capably handle this matter unless the perpetrator fled to Washington, DC, or, worse yet, Mexico.

I ask you this question: if someone in your family were harmed by a crime that is not terrorism-related, would you want the ability to ask the FBI for help or input? You may not be able to in the near future. Worse yet, if you ask the FBI now, they will say that they will investigate, but in reality, your case will sit behind any terrorism matter. That terrorism matter may be the leftover chalk wiped from your grade-schooler's chalkboard that his teacher believed might be anthrax. Prioritize, look at the statistics, and do not make all decisions based on fear.

When you have cancer, your battle against this nemesis must be an extremely important focus. When the cancer is at its most virulent points, the patient's efforts to fight it will be his or her number one priority. Yet even at the most bleak and darkest moments, the cancer should never be your only focal point. Everything must still continue in some type of balance. While dealing with cancer, you must still spend time with your family, enjoy recreation, and continue to work (if feasible), and so on. Those who put everything on hold while dealing with cancer and treatments do themselves a disservice. When human beings are completely removed from their normal routines, the body knows that something is amiss. Ten to fifteen years ago, cancer patients were routinely placed in cancer units, ostensibly for care, but more realistically as a safe place to die. Today, doctors and hospitals make every attempt to get the cancer patient out of the hospital and home as quickly as possible.

After I returned from Saudi Arabia and had serious brain injury symptoms, my oncologists and surgeons rapidly determined the issues and problems specific to me. From being aware of nothing more than that I was experiencing headaches, impaired vision, and disorientation, in only three weeks, my doctors completed the following:

1. Drained the excessive blood from my brain to relieve pressure.
2. Determined I had two major tumors inside my head, performed biopsies on them, and found them to be malignant.
3. Conducted numerous diagnostic tests in other regions of my body, searching for other cancerous sites (they found two).
4. Treated me with medication to limit pain and tumor growth.
5. Completed open-brain surgery to remove the tumors from my head.
6. Finished Gamma Knife (pinpoint radiation therapy) through my skull and into my brain to irradiate the areas where the tumors had been.
7. Conducted diagnostic testing to determine results and options.
8. Provided outstanding informational data and support to me and my family.
9. Served me some fairly unappetizing food and sent me home.

Steps 1 through 9 above took place over two and a half weeks, and I was probably only hospitalized as an inpatient for a total of five or six days. Following my brain surgery, I remained in the hospital for two additional days. These doctors were so confident and competent that they cut out a chunk of my skull, went into my brain, sliced away two huge tumors that were bleeding, closed me up, and sent me home to Mama in under three full days. Wow! Additionally, this was done with a full team of doctors, not just one person. There were surgeons, oncologists, specialists, Gamma Knife experts, radiation technicians, therapists, anesthesiologists, nurses, ad infinitum. It was handled like a battle scene from *Star Trek,* and there was nothing out of place. It was inspiring to observe the functioning of these teams of doctors and support staff. The entire time they completed their tasks, they were caring, personable, and generally wonderful human beings. All this was done under the highest degrees of stress imaginable—one screw-up and a patient could be paralyzed, mentally incapacitated, or dead.

When an FBI employee considers the responsibility that a doctor must bear on a routine basis, it should be evident that the FBI job is not as damn difficult as we try to make it out to be. FBI pontificators who drone on endlessly about the importance of our mission in the war against terrorism are only blowing their own horns. There are people in this country who complete a job that is overwhelmingly more important than chasing a bad guy. Doctors save, and extend, the lives of tens of thousands of people every year. All the law enforcement and intelligence agencies combined impact only a miniscule fraction of that number.

I do not attempt in the above statements to minimize what the FBI does in criminal and terrorism investigations. I only try to place it in an appropriate overall historical and personal perspective. The thousands of lives lost to terrorism, both here and abroad, are tragic losses, yet compared to the tens of thousands taken by the enemy of cancer, the threat of al-Qaeda is pretty meek. If the Zen gods (though Zen does not have gods in the traditional sense) put me in charge for a day, one of the first things I would do is eliminate cancer. Cancer takes far too many purely innocent people. While innocent victims suffer the fate of terrorist attacks as well, at least there is potential retribution by the victims' government. With cancer, there is no one to blame. The bureau should not overemphasize its own importance in the war against terrorist entities. This duty should only be one in many of my organization's functions. It is presumptuous of our management structure to restyle the FBI into an internal CIA. The American public seeks protection from terror but also protection from the other things that will injure them physically, financially, and socially. For the FBI to blithely follow a road where terrorism is the stated (or implicitly indicated) only route is absolute folly. This singular path is made doubly dubious because of why it was taken. The events of September 11 necessitated a change in focus but not a complete restructuring of how an entire criminal investigative agency functioned. I am an advocate of change, versatility, and innovation. The FBI is fully capable of handling the two-fold responsibility of fighting terrorism while continuing to successfully investigate traditional criminal activity. Investigating traditional crime should not take a backseat to terrorism in today's FBI. The balance should be a sliding scale as it always has been in FBI history.

The terrorism side of the FBI correctly advocates that the bureau be provided additional resources to fight terrorism and traditional criminal violations. To date, Congress has not provided us sufficient resources to quadruple the size of the FBI, and it is clear Congress does not intend to provide us with that level of funding. In fact, there is some motion in Congress to dismantle the FBI and create a new agency. When incidents occur (and intelligence is developed) that one particular area of criminal activity is more egregious or growing rapidly, it should be targeted and resisted. If a criminal activity conversely seems to be decreasing in intensity, enforcement should be decreased. These priorities should be considered in the context of what the American public wants the FBI to do. It is quite likely that immediately after the terrorist attacks, the public would want virtually all the bureau's resources targeted to that terrorist event (we did that). Now we have had few major terrorist incidents in the states recently. Does the public want the majority of FBI resources spent on terrorism? It is more likely that they want the bureau to be able to respond to multiple threats as is demanded by the certain specific criminal activities around the country.

As an example, if you reside in Colorado, and your ten-year-old child is lured via the Internet to Wyoming and is the victim of sexual assault, the FBI's investigative program of investigating Internet sexual predators will be very important to you. If all the FBI emphasizes is counterterrorism, this interstate crime against your child may go uninvestigated and unresolved. Someone as a citizen viewing from the outside may see terrorism as the FBI's primary focus. Yet this is partially a media phenomenon. If too many resources are shifted to terrorism, who will investigate parental kidnappings, massive bank frauds, Internet violations, stock manipulation, fugitive murders, Internet pornography, etc.? Any victim of these crimes (and numerous others) will want and expect the experience and expertise of the FBI. To deny these victims such assistance would be no different from limiting the FBI's assistance to the victims of the terrorist acts of September 11. The strength of the FBI is to respond to crisis. To administratively limit the ability to provide such assistance shows weakness and fear on the part of the management of the FBI. It is correct, as the director has advocated, that the FBI's job in the terrorist world is prevention and not response. Yet much of what we will continue to do in the terrorism arena is merely respond.

It is unconscionable for the FBI to abandon (or even minimize) its responsibilities in areas other than terrorism. We must provide superlative service to the American public in multiple and divergent areas. It is conceivable that the FBI will need additional resources, and if this is so, they should be expeditiously provided. Just as cancer patients seek out specialists for their specific type of cancer, victims of specific crimes should be able to approach the FBI and believe they will deal with bureau experts in the fields of drugs, kidnapping, or Internet fraud and not just a terrorism agent dabbling in a case on his day off.

> We got too many gangsters doing dirty deeds,
> We've got too much corruption, too much crime
> in the streets,
> It's time the long arm of the law put a few more
> in the ground,
> Send 'em all to their maker and he'll settle 'em down,
> Justice is the one thing you should always find
> You got to saddle up your boys,
> You got to draw a hard line,
> When the gun smoke settles we'll sing a victory tune,
> We'll all meet back at the local saloon,
> We'll raise up our glasses against evil forces,
> Singing whiskey for my men, beer for my horses.
> —From "Beer for My Horses"
> *by Toby Keith*

Set out in full text below is an e-mail sent out to all FBI employees on May 20, 2002, from Director Mueller explaining how the priorities of the FBI were being revamped and reevaluated. Any agent who had been working traditional criminal matters correctly interpreted this e-mail as indicating they were now a second-class employee in the FBI and their work will no longer continue to be valued or supported. From the moment of Mueller's ascendancy to the top of the FBI, it has been both stated and unstated that resources (in both money and staffing) will be directed primarily to counterterrorism. If, as an employee, you are involved in investigating violations other than counterterrorism, you will be forced to do what you can with whatever resources remain. As one final note before I reprint the full e-mail, I comment on the director's phrase "the world has changed." He justifies an entire dismantling of the FBI's organizational structure because of 9/11. Had the world actually changed? Absolutely not! The seeds of terrorism groups such as al-Qaeda had been present and known to the intelligence community for years. The world had not changed. One terrorist group had just been victorious in one isolated incident. However devastating that loss was for this country, 9/11 will exact more damage if it forces the FBI to abandon its duty to protect citizens in areas other than terrorism.

Director Mueller's e-mail dated May 20, 2002, stated as follows:

> TO ALL EMPLOYEES:
>
> Since my arrival at the FBI, I have been working to define FBI priorities—priorities that will shape our operations and the deployment of our resources. These reflect input from several SAC conferences, from meetings with the Advisory Groups, from many of you as I have traveled around the country, from other federal, state and local law enforcement agencies, from Congress, and from many others, and I greatly appreciated the many constructive suggestions I have received throughout this process.
>
> In my own mind, I wanted these priorities to be simple and clear—a list of our top challenges that we all agree on and will work toward. There are no surprises on the list, but each will require changes in the way we do business.
>
> Here are the ten:
>
> 1. Protect the United States from terrorist attack.
> 2. Protect the United States against foreign intelligence operations and espionage.
> 3. Protect the United States against cyber-based attacks and high technology crimes.
> 4. Combat public corruption at all levels.
> 5. Protect civil rights.
> 6. Combat transnational and national criminal organizations and enterprises.
> 7. Combat major white-collar crime.
> 8. Combat significant violent crime.
> 9. Support federal, state, county, municipal, and international partners.
> 10. Upgrade technology to successfully perform the FBI's mission.
>
> Let me take them from the top.
>
> The first three are our most critical challenges. They are not new priorities, but they are different in 2002 because the world has changed—and each requires new ways of thinking and doing.

Our goal in counter-terrorism is prevention. It is not, as in the past, reacting to attacks with excellence and bringing terrorists to justice. Our goal is prevention. That does not mean that prosecution is not important. Prosecution is an absolutely critical element of prevention. But making clear that the goal is prevention rather than prosecution will mean less focus on traditional law enforcement operations and much more on intelligence and analysis. Also counter-terrorism is the top priority of every single field office and of every component of headquarters that supports these efforts in any way. This means a constant need to reassess—and as necessary shift—resources to address counter-terrorism. We will need to be more flexible and agile in addressing the constantly shifting terrorism threat. Our enemy is not static and we must not be either.

Likewise, I expect our counterintelligence functions to be transformed: elevated in importance, controlled on a national level, and given a profoundly changed strategy and focus—not simply trying to keep a close eye on those trying to steal the secrets as we have done in the past: but rather working to build walls around our Nation's secrets and most valuable assets. We must openly acknowledge that we have had recent failures in this area and we must learn from them. Like counter-terrorism, the costs of even a single successful "attack" can be devastating.

Our cyber program must both protect against cyber attacks and also investigate high-technology frauds and other crimes. It is going to require resources and energy to get us to the cutting edge in these areas, but we must do it. In this area—as in everything we do—our goal must be to be the very best in the world.

The next five priorities are traditional areas of responsibility: public corruption, civil rights, national and international organized crime groups and enterprises, white-collar crime, and violent crime. All are extremely important to our mission and to the safety of the American people. But we will closely focus our resources on major crimes in the areas of white-collar, organized, and violent crime, where we are able to make unique law enforcement contributions. Even with the abundant new resources Congress has provided us, we must be more sharply focused to ensure we always are giving our top priorities every necessary resource. The stakes are too high to do otherwise.

The final two priorities are not programs, but rather the crucial infrastructure for all our investigative operation. Without federal, state, county, municipal, and international cooperation, our relatively small numbers of investigators cannot possibly begin to gather sufficient intelligence or evidence in any of our priority programs—we have about 28,000 employees and there are over 600,000 state and local law enforcement officers in this country alone. Obviously we cannot begin to do the job alone. Without technology upgrades, we cannot communicate; we cannot share information; we cannot begin to make sense of the intelligence and evidence that we do collect. We are working hard to get you the technology you need to do your jobs. I know many of you are assisting in that effort—helping us design the right system. Unfortunately, this will take some time. But we are absolutely committed to getting this done and done right, and Congress is providing the money to enable us to do so.

I am satisfied that these ten priorities capture what we must do to achieve our mission and to protect the United States from attack and Americans from harm. They will require reorganizing and retooling and, above all, continued flexibility and innovation by all of us. Some of the changes will be difficult. They will require changes in how each of us does our job. But the FBI is the finest law enforcement organization in the world and the reason for that is you: its employees. We must all continue to hold ourselves to the standard of excellence—ceaselessly working to do our jobs even better so that we will be the best in the world at whatever we do. Never before has the country depended on us so heavily. I know that we are up to the challenge.

The beginning of the demolition of the FBI had begun and the first gauntlet laid down; employees bureau-wide cringed. What can be anticipated as the primary destructive forces likely to be present in our next-generation FBI if the organization proceeds to lumber down this path of destruction?

THE FBI CANNOT EVEN BEGIN TO FIGHT TERRORISM EFFECTIVELY IF WE VIEW TERRORISM AS HAVING A DIRECT LINKAGE TO THE RELIGION OF ISLAM

When discussing terrorism, the FBI drones on eternally about organizations such as al-Qaeda, the Taliban, or other groups. Realistically, however, many adherents to a terrorist mind-set are no more organized than a college fraternity party. Many individuals who commit random and violent actions are, instead, driven by a twisted overriding mentality of hating Western civilization and the United States. Many of the perpetrators of these crimes are funded by organized terrorist entities and counseled on what activity might be most disruptive. They are not commanded by Osama bin Laden's underlings to run planes into buildings. A general possible concept is formulated, and the idea is handed over to adherents of the group to plan and actualize. It is true that on other occasions, individuals are provided specific training and logistical support by an organization like al-Qaeda and are well organized.

> One must become as humble as the dust,
> before he can discover the truth.
> —*Mahatma Gandhi*

The compartmentalization of terrorists is what creates success and limits risk. In the broadest sense, the leaders of the group may merely state that the United States is the Great Satan and must be destroyed. This methodology leaves the means of disruption up to the individual fanatic. Or the command can be narrower—kill American military. Periodically, the edict can be even more specific by providing actual plans, funding, and logistical support (the 9/11 attacks).

One of the areas where the FBI has begun to have success is that when dealing with terrorists, we should not view them all as killers and suicide bombers. The traditional American depiction of a terrorist as a Farsi-speaking, turban-wearing religious zealot is often inaccurate. The Middle Eastern culture is extremely ethnically and culturally diverse in its own right. The countries of Saudi Arabia, Iraq, Iran, and others have a history that literally dwarfs anything to which the United States might lay claim. These countries had organized language, culture, and religion centuries prior to the West. The divergence here is remarkable between what the typical American believes and actual fact. While many Middle Eastern countries are poor by American standards (for instance, Iraq or Iran), many are remarkably modern and advanced (for instance, Saudi Arabia or Egypt), yet the media in the West plays up the differences between our cultures rather than the similarities. Even the FBI feeds on this somewhat and tends to view Islamic groups in the United States as questionable.

The actual religion of Islam is the most tolerant of all adherent faiths. The religious tome of the Koran is the only primary religious writing that specifically states other religions should be respected and endorsed (you will not find that tolerance in any Bible you pick up). The differences Americans perceive as so radical (such as females wearing an abaya, the covering black gown with a hood and veil) are only holdovers from a bygone era. When I was in Riyadh, I took great pleasure in shopping and watching the women in their abayas. They would be covered head to ankle, but you could still see the Nike running shoes and the bottoms of American jeans. Moreover, the Mabahith (the Saudi counterparts to FBI or CIA) told me that as soon as everyone gets to their houses, most, except the most traditional, strip down to T-shirts and watch TV just like over here. Yes, they do bow to Mecca multiple times each day, but still they do the same things you and I do, perhaps with a little more piety. Imagine Mormons with less tithe to the church, but fancier clothing (some of the abayas are embroidered and gorgeous).

The culture of many of the terrorist regions is superlative in form and design. As Americans, we must realize that generally, while viewed with curiosity in the Middle East, we are not disliked, and law enforcement must do everything possible to educate themselves about the history and culture of Eastern regions. Repeatedly, while working in Riyadh, I would receive leads from FBI field offices in the United States asking something like, "Albany has identified Muslim Omar Mohammed as having been born in Jeddah, Saudi Arabia, on May 19, 1964. This individual subsequently relocated to a suburb of Albany and is attending evening classes at State University of New York, working on his agricultural engineering degree. Riyadh is requested to immediately provide all background on this individual and fully identify any and all ties to al-Qaeda or other terrorist groups." That lead demonstrates the still-present stupidity and cultural backwardness of how some in the FBI view terrorism. The FBI could clearly use a few courses in Middle Eastern history so all our employees do not equate being an Arab Muslim with being a terrorist. Many Westerners are horrified at how women are treated in the Middle East. I agree that how women are dealt with seems inappropriate to me as a Westerner, but that is neither my country nor my culture.

To fight actual terrorism, we need to identify it and determine if there is radical discourse by the Imam (priest) at the mosque. Then we should speak to the Imam and ask how the FBI can help him get the word out to Muslims and non-Muslims. The FBI needs to work proactively with the leaders in the Muslim and Arab communities. The FBI must understand how the Muslim community is interacting in the region. Think of it as a citizens' academy for Muslims. Demonstrate repeatedly and frequently via interaction that the FBI can assist the Muslim community. Through this cooperation and trust, the FBI may begin to garner the faith of the community and also identify people willing to assist if terrorism or other criminal activity is initiated.

THE FBI CANNOT FIGHT TERRORISM IF WE NARROWLY CONSTRUE TERRORISM AS VIOLENT ACTS

Terrorism, in a broad construct, is one group making efforts to disrupt a government via unlawful means. The FBI must construe terrorism broadly, and to combat the terrorists, we must utilize multiple investigative routes and not merely terrorism statutes. Many terrorism laws are very narrow. Examples would be plotting or actually conducting terrorist acts or providing funding or material assistance to similar projects. Often, the assistance is very subtle. Making reservations for a terrorist-linked individual to fly into the United States, providing a bank account, or obtaining an apartment for meetings are typical examples of assistance. The FBI must be vigilant for actions that seem suspicious even though not illegal when planned or conducted.

In medicine, it is an overriding concept that the body must be viewed holistically. You do not treat just one aspect of a cancer. The entire body is treated and hopefully healed in total by a complete eradication of the cancer. The patient's specific health problems are prioritized and then treated in order of severity. For complete health, the entire body must become well. Oncologists are beginning to realize that without the proper mental preparation and care, even if the cancer is surgically removed, it can develop elsewhere if not considered with complete health as the overriding goal. To remain cancer-free, we must stay healthy.

The FBI is similar. Even if we identify the perpetrators of 9/11, we must continue to identify all persons even tangentially tied to the criminal group to monitor their progress. We may not possess the evidence to indict or convict, but we must locate these sites so they can be watched just like a dormant cancer. Additionally, the conduct we monitor must be broad and extend beyond violent acts, financing, liaison, and overheard conversations. We as the FBI cannot wait for violence to occur before we begin to watch. The key counterpoint to this vigilance is an immediate ability to back off if nothing is actually there. The FBI should conduct massive and intensive waves of investigation against groups and individuals at the slightest possibility of terrorism activity. If terrorism activity is suspected, major and intrusive investigative techniques should quickly be authorized. However, if initial investigation shows nothing, then the matter should quickly be dropped. For example, it is inexcusable to do extended wiretaps on targets when overhears do not indicate criminal conduct. The FBI routinely runs overhears for months at a time during which minimal or no criminal activity is intercepted. The FBI should get in the process of quickly targeting potential subjects by limiting the difficulties to initiate an investigation, then pushing hard with the case during the initial stages. If the case continues to make good strides, push forward on all cylinders, but if the case is not moving, immediately close the investigation. The public will not feel violated if an incorrect target is investigated and the matter is quickly closed. We as the FBI must be vigilant for much more than violent terrorist action, and we must be ready to close those investigations just as rapidly. It is important to understand that pertinent overhears may be intelligence data. It may be very valuable to learn that Mr. A is doing a legitimate business deal with Samir because it establishes a documented connection. This may be very true if Samir is a documented terrorist associate.

WHEN DETERMINING HOW TO ADDRESS TERRORISM, THE FBI IS NOT APPROPRIATELY CONSIDERING THE INPUT OF THE RANK-AND-FILE INVESTIGATORS

The FBI is being played like a fiddle by headquarter employees whose only goal is to forward the cause of a terrorism agenda. Everyone now at HQ and Quantico is espousing the absolute importance of terrorism cases at the expense of all else. This is being done because many of the HQ "empty suits" are only saying what they know their superiors want to hear. If you speak to HQ personnel and supervisors individually, almost all agree we are over focusing our resources on terrorism. Unfortunately, because they all have careers, they refuse to openly speak out against the terrorism party line because it is not what the director wants to hear. The rank-and-file employees must not be scared, and they must repeatedly advise upper management of the error of the current path. To do any less is dishonest to the vow we took when we accepted the job as FBI agents. Merely because HQ and management are weak, other employees do not have to knuckle under. Every opportunity to talk to management is a chance to advise that the bureau must continue to be challenged by more than the one facet of terrorism cases. In our darkest of moments, when we as an organization teeter on the brink of no return, each employee must speak openly of the error of our present path. We can find our way back to the correct path of a diversified and multifaceted agency with depth of purpose, but we better do it soon.

> I cannot find my way, there is no star in all the
> shrouded heavens anywhere and there is not a whisper
> in the air of any living voice, But one so far that
> I can hear it only as a bar of lost imperial music.
> —Edwin Arlington Robinson

A profoundly lost feeling is what a cancer patient feels. Identification with goals can establish a new and different focus in a cancer victim's life. Cancer patients must refocus on new goals in both family and health to assist them in their time of depression. To become strong and steady of purpose, cancer victims must reestablish these new goals. Internally, examine goals you desired to achieve but set aside due to the time constraints of a job or a personal relationship. Then develop a plan and try to accomplish these newly identified ambitions. If you are successful in these, at this roughest of moments, the satisfaction will be great. In much the same way, the FBI can overcome our dramatic overemphasis on terrorism, and our employees can return stronger for achieving during a period when the deck has been stacked against us by our very own leadership.

DIFFERENT EMPLOYEES FEAR DIFFERENT THINGS, BUT OVERALL, THE FBI SHOULD TRY TO ELIMINATE ITS CULTURE OF FEAR

When the FBI first began to emphasize terrorism at the expense of all other violations, I believed I would be a useless dinosaur unable to contribute to our new terrorism mission. What I determined instead was that it was the foreign counterintelligence (FCI) and international terrorism (IT) houses that held ingrained institutional fear. Before 9/11, there had rarely been occasions where either FCI or IT had to move rapidly. Because spies and terrorists planned their activity over long periods of time, the FBI rarely needed a sense of time urgency on these cases. Additionally, due to federal legal procedures, the process for obtaining authorizations was excruciatingly slow.

Accordingly, terrorism investigations generally proceeded at a snaillike pace. The incidents of the first World Trade Center bombing, and more influentially 9/11, changed the pace of the game. Once the speed of investigation changed, many traditional FCI and IT types became fish out of water. They were unable to move rapidly in investigations and were sometimes stalled unilaterally at HQ because they could not keep up with the rapid developments.

Therefore, agents with traditional criminal investigative backgrounds were often brought in to inject energy into such cases. Criminal investigators were familiar with short deadlines, limited preparation time for testimony, and rushing about in general. Now the FBI was experiencing a twofold "fear" dilemma. The criminal agents now working terrorism were concerned because they did not fully understand the legal violations, and the terrorism FCI types were scared because their slower pace was unsuited to rapidly developing criminal-style matters.

> When you find yourself overpowered,
> as it were, by melancholy, the best way is to go out,
> and do something kind to somebody or other.
> —*Keble*

To eliminate the fears, clear explanations of duties should have been explained to both agent groups (those familiar with criminal and those knowledgeable of terrorism). While halfheartedly attempted, this was not done efficiently. After my first brain surgery, I was cognitively not myself. It was the first time in my life I was scared. Death never terrified me, nor pain, nor most of the things many people are concerned with. Once my mental faculties returned, the treatment options were discussed and all risks were explained: hair loss, tremors, death, and dementia. My decision was easy: do whatever you think will be most likely to produce success no matter how painful or unpleasant, but do not turn me into a vegetable.

I believe the choice for the FBI is similarly clear. To eliminate its culture of fear, IT and FCI employees should be integrated with criminal personnel on a fifty-fifty basis. One terrorism guy with a criminal partner should work jointly on a case hand in hand, regardless if the investigation is criminal or terrorist. They will learn each other's skills and draw upon each other's talents. In two to three years, both should continue as partners and switch to the other side (IT/FCI if criminal before or vice versa). After this cycle of training and case management, our culture of fear of the unknown will have diminished significantly.

WE FAIL TO SHARE INFORMATION WITH OTHER AGENCIES (BUT WE ARE GETTING BETTER)

When I entered the FBI almost twenty years ago, the FBI often tried to rule the sandbox, and we did not always play fairly with other agencies. My supervisors in Las Vegas and Los Angeles routinely misled DEA and local law enforcement on my drug cases, and DEA and the locals lied to us even more frequently. To run successful cases, individual agents needed to personally know someone at the corresponding agency they could contact and trust. Fortunately, over the last two decades, the FBI has made a concerted effort to resolve this petty foolishness. The FBI began to form task forces and to fully share information, sources, and manpower with local police departments, DEA, ATF, and other agencies. I was fortunate to be a participant in a number of these task forces. While sometimes jealousies did exist, the overwhelming impact was positive. Some of the penultimate cases in which I was involved were these types of task force environments.

When I first began to have dealing with our FBI terrorism people, shortly after 9/11, I was flabbergasted they often had a terrible relationship with CIA and NSA. I learned that there was virtually no sharing of information, and on each case, both would try to claim all the credit. I was told the jealousy was entrenched on both sides, and both agencies were set up for big-time black eyes. Now the public understands how minimally the CIA and FBI talked prior to and shortly after 9/11. The credibility of both agencies was harmed significantly. One of the principal reasons for the lack of cooperation was that both agencies were so backward in technology that they could not have watched a fox in a henhouse. Accordingly, whenever either received a tidbit of relevant information, they guarded it with all their might. Additionally, both agencies believed they were still working in the 1970s and 1980s, monitoring spies from the Eastern Bloc. Another unfortunate reality during the time before and shortly after 9/11 was both the CIA and FBI believed there were legal restraints and walls that prohibited the sharing of intelligence information. Probably the best thing 9/11 did was to allow the intelligence community to eliminate some of these walls.

Set out below is a quotation from an article entitled "If the Spooks Can't Analyze Their Own Data, Why Call It Intelligence?" written by John Perry Darlow for *Forbes ASAP* magazine on October 7, 2002.

> *After a decade of both fighting with and consulting to the intelligence community, I've concluded that the American intelligence system is broken beyond repair, self-protective beyond reform, and permanently fixated on a world that no longer exists... The most distressing discovery... was the almost universal frustration of employees at the intransigence of the beast they inhabited. They felt forced into incompetence by information hoarding and non-communication, both within the CIA and other related agencies. They hated their primitive technology. They felt unappreciated, oppressed, demoralized.*

The above quotation is an honest assessment of how the CIA (or the FBI for that matter) malfunctioned. As with the FBI, individual employees were periodically able to battle through obstruction and lack of support to achieve success. It just did not happen very often.

Eventually, it became clear that this system was so irretrievably broken that it had to be scrapped after 9/11. The congressional hearings and intelligence inquiries demonstrated that we not only failed to share information between agencies but we also often did not share it with the appropriate people in our own agency. Amazingly, the government is correctable: since the fallout, the FBI and the other intelligence groups are beginning to work together. I use an analogy that the CIA and FBI are similar to cats and dogs. They look and act very differently. Some people like one or the other, some like neither, and some appreciate both. Each has unique skills of tracking or chasing, fighting or hiding, and biting or scratching. The FBI and CIA work together. While I am still not sure that we are cozy enough that we will be licking each other's fur clean, we have come a long way.

THE FBI IS NOT MALLEABLE ENOUGH TO FIGHT UP-AND-COMING TERRORIST GROUPS

The FBI by its own design is limited in flexibility because of its bureaucratic nature. It is difficult to be successful in the FBI even when investigating huge slow-moving criminal enterprises. It is undeniably more difficult when you are working against terrorist groups, which, while well organized, are often amorphous and mercurial. To eliminate this weakness, the FBI must continue to push through new ideas and change even if this flies directly in the face of our agency inertia.

In cancer treatment, you are often offered multiple types of treatment. No single treatment is correct for everyone. Each person must obtain multiple opinions from different doctors and weigh all the relevant opinions. With most cancers, you will have sufficient time to meet with various types of oncologists because very few types of cancer are immediate life-or-death emergencies. Once you assess each treatment option, you can then consider all the pros and cons, both as related to the cancer and to your overall well-being.

Being organized when deciding how to fight terrorism does not preclude being innovative and versatile. An innovative idea is just one more option posited as a possible attack plan against a certain terrorist group. The FBI too often sees only what it expects to see. We expect to see only terrorists helping to finance terrorists but have found this to be inaccurate. Legitimate businessmen, both in the United States and abroad, will deal with terrorist tentacles if it brings in income. This is why the bureau must be flexible enough to foresee new ways of moving currency, weapons, or personnel. I would suggest that the FBI have brainstorming sessions with their terrorist experts and ask, "If I were a terrorist, how could I most efficiently strike fear into the United States?" Log the answers and do some proactive work to guard against such incidents. Director Mueller is trying with his new "ten priorities" to give the organization direction, but I believe it was completed backward. We inside the FBI know our priorities are skewed and probably are unmanageable. Now as an organization, we must identify a long-term game plan that incorporates our basic organizational whole. The game plan should eventually take us to the point where a possibility of success exists. With cancer, that position is hopefully remission, a cure, or at a minimum, some pleasurable remaining existence. My suggestion for the FBI in terrorism matters is to be extraordinarily organized and then brainstorm radical solution paths when no answers are readily apparent. Here are a few potential solutions to the issues created by Director Mueller's new terrorism-based FBI.

Formalize Organizational Processes to Reduce the Conflict between Needing Innovation to Stimulate New Ideas and Maintaining Structure to Provide Stability

It seems illogical that one could create innovation by formalizing procedures, but it can be achieved. In an organization like the FBI, some employees must be told to come up with new ideas. Many employees will not do anything different unless specifically told to do so. I can tell an agent to go interview terrorist associate Abdul, and 90 percent would probably interview him in the traditional FBI interview format. If I want it done differently, I as the case agent must tell the interviewer the different manner in which I want it handled or, at a minimum, advise that this is an unusual situation and it may need the interviewer's imagination. It is always good to have a plan in terrorism investigations; we just need to keep our minds open to divergent possible routes the case may take. You can never be too innovative or strange when considering possible questions or options. The interviewer may never go into these areas, but at least he has considered them as possible options.

In cancer treatment, doctors set out detailed logistical charts explaining a patient's alternatives regarding procedures. However, doctors then sometimes provide wild and crazy final experimental treatment options like being injected with hamster ovary secretions. Set out below is a chart found in *Understanding Cancer* by C. Norman Coleman, MD.

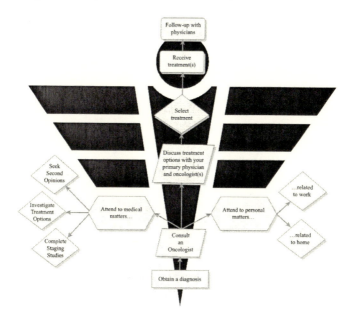

The chart is a schematic for how to logically and dispassionately begin to assess treatment options for cancer. A similar module could be utilized to select investigative strategies in terrorism matters. The importance is that the structure provided should be comforting to the patient (or investigator), but the structure does not limit or impede groundbreaking thought under the "investigate treatment options" category. You can organize and still be innovative both in cancer and FBI terrorism methodology.

Instead of Utilizing Wholesale Deportation of Terrorist Associates, Consideration Should Be Given to Having America's Ways Co-opt Them by Allowing Them to Remain the United States

I am aware that the above solution will not work in every case. Many terrorist associates who have relocated to the United States remain hard-core advocates for their terrorist organizations. In fact, for some of these individuals, simply observing the freedom of the hedonistic culture in America can become another spur to conduct terrorist activities. There is, however, another group of relocated terrorist sympathizers who, when they come to the United States, quickly become Americanized and part ways with terrorist activity. America is a very open and free culture, particularly for females, compared to the rest of the world. In the more traditional Arab countries, there is no alcohol, no premarital sex, and limited fun. In the United States, we have dance clubs, topless-dancing establishments, and alcohol on demand. Frequently, after the initial overwhelming rush of the experience, traditional Muslim Arabs begin to be co-opted by our wicked ways. This is true for terrorist associates as well.

They may come to the United States, believing it is the American devil, but after a time, they start to somewhat enjoy at least parts of America's version of Hedonism II. Once influenced in this manner, the likelihood of these terrorist-linked individuals committing terrorist acts here is greatly diminished. Among their peers, they may still toss out fiery rhetoric now and again, but actual criminal acts are unlikely.

> As civilization progresses,
> we should improve our laws basically,
> not superficially.
> Many things that are lawful
> are highly immoral,
> and some things which are moral
> are unlawful.
> —*Henry L. Doherty*

After the 9/11 incidents in New York and at the Pentagon, a number of individuals in Phoenix were identified as being linked to the terrorists' families. Extensive work was done by the Phoenix office to determine if the linkage was coincidental or if the people remaining in Phoenix might have had knowledge of the 9/11 plot. I do not know that any conclusions were reached because the targets (if they could appropriately be called that) returned to the Middle East. My purpose in providing the example is that some of these targets went to nude-dancing clubs, drank, and spent plenty of time dating American women. After more in-depth investigation, it became clear that we had little to fear from our Americanized subgroup. However, some of the others presented a significant risk to America's safety; they were already gone but subsequently legally banned from the United States. The FBI and all aspects of US Homeland Security must continue to carefully monitor immigrants in this country to ensure they have no terrorism nexus. Still, my guess is that their stay in America will change many. And if you are watching the strippers at Buck's Topless Bar and you meet Samir, who is an exchange student from Yemen, welcome him to the United States and buy him a beer. You might make a new friend and help save your country at the same time.

While We Have Made Significant Strides to Work with the CIA, We Need to Fully Integrate with Them for Complete Success

The FBI's relationship with the CIA, both in the United States and overseas, has improved dramatically since 9/11. One of Director Mueller's greatest accomplishments is that the FBI is more efficiently sharing information with the CIA, NSA, and all the other intelligence agencies. Still, we can go much further down our path of cooperation. As the entertainer Pink would say, "Let's get this party started!" There should never be an occasion where competition with the CIA should lead to conflict. The FBI's mission is different from the CIA's, and we should be able to work together. The CIA is designed to combat espionage and terrorism via operations overseas, and the FBI is designed to protect domestic security within the States. However, the CIA must also conduct activity here in the States, and the FBI must also be operational overseas to complement each agency's primary missions.

In other words, both the FBI and CIA need to work effectively throughout the world. When the CIA is successful, it can only help the FBI, and the reverse is also true. The competition can be eliminated easily by completely and routinely sharing information. This will also limit duplication of effort and utilize the skills of the most knowledgeable people in each agency. In intelligence agencies, information tends to be hoarded, and this practice, which was fortified during the Cold War, must be halted.

Much of intelligence work is based on the "need to know" concept. Unless there is a reason I need to know about your investigation (for example, I have a related case), I should never hear about it. The concept was that a "need to know" screen limited the number of people familiar with the investigation, and therefore, fewer people were in a position to leak the information or inadvertently disclose it. The intelligence community, and the FBI and CIA in particular, must eliminate the "need to know" concept as it now exists. In the alternative, an entire group of employees should be actively familiar with most all the major intelligence initiatives and investigations. It would literally require thousands of such employees due to the volumes of investigative and intelligence data being developed. These employees would then be analytical repositories for the information and parcel it out to the actual investigators. Additionally, investigators could query these employees (and their computers) whenever new information was developed. This "gatekeeper" concept would allow a small group of employees to be privy to a stockpile of valuable information, and then their only function would be to distribute it to the appropriate FBI field office or CIA posting. There would be no difference between CIA or FBI information. The gatekeepers would be in receipt of all information from both agencies and would forward it to whichever agency could most efficiently handle it. Ah, cooperation at last.

Even if You Feel Betrayed by the FBI'S Switch to Terrorism, Do Not Give Up

While I clearly believe the FBI's wholesale move to antiterrorism is an error, I will never stop trying. And Mr. Mueller will not be the director forever. While he may not allow the organization to return to its appropriate roots as a dual-purpose criminal/terrorism agency, the subsequent director may. Many within the organization (even in the upper reaches of management) understand the mistake the director is making. Upon his departure, things may very well change.

Many current employees feel lost and angry that the FBI is now "terrorism central." Lost and angry is the same way many feel when diagnosed with cancer. The person should try to avoid this slippery slope by attempting to obtain all available information. Go to cancer websites and cancer therapy groups. Do whatever it takes. Make success against this cancer a high priority, and emphasize your own well-being as a central issue. Keep striving to locate a path that will take you through the cancer's emotional toll. The physical side you can impact by diligently selecting the best physicians. But if you give up and stop trying, all is lost. Even though you may feel a betrayal by being diagnosed with cancer or having a promising criminal investigation discontinued in lieu of a minor terrorism tidbit, never stop trying. Give 100 percent effort.

> In the middle of the journey of our life, I found myself
> in a dark wood, where the straight path was lost.
> —The Divine Comedy, *Dante*

While employees of the FBI may feel betrayed by Mueller's change of focus midstream, we have no other choice but to continue to try and to adapt. We must go with the flow of change to continue to contribute positively to the organization. That does not mean we need to roll over and compromise our integrity. When salmon swim upstream, they periodically take breaks by resting in swirling pools along the river's edge. In those moments, the salmon are in the best moments of their world. They are completing their destiny by swimming upstream to spawn, but they are also taking a second to enjoy a moment in time. In the FBI, many employees are fighting upstream to continue to complete the important task of criminal investigations, which are now perceived as bastard stepchildren. At this same time, we can be confident that times will change. If we as the unwanted criminal investigators continue to complete good work, the scale may shift back. If the pendulum swings back to non-terrorism investigations, the criminal side of the FBI must be prepared to run at full speed. To be prepared, the old guard criminal investigative types need to maintain their skills and be diligent. When the switch back occurs, it may occur quickly. Remember, failure to prepare is preparing to fail.

CONCLUSION

The CIA and FBI often allow internal jealousy to interfere with their true work. I believe cooperation is improving in this area, and full access to each other's data via gatekeepers is an excellent option. When people require cancer treatment, they must proceed through specific organizational steps to ensure they will receive the best treatment. If you have lymphoma, go to a lymphoma specialist; if melanoma, seek out that expert. In the FBI, we should not allow our agency to lose its experts on criminal matters because, once gone, it will be difficult to locate qualified replacements. Overemphasizing terrorism cases to the exclusion of all else will diminish our skill base and limit our subsequent flexibility. Surprisingly, focusing only on terrorism will also make us less capable in that area as well. A diversity of experience is what rounds out and solidifies an employee's confidence. The FBI is setting itself up to fail if we become an internal CIA.

In cancer therapy books, repeated reference is made to providing appropriate care to those patients in the final stages of cancer who are in the "dying time"—patients whose cancer has progressed too far along to be treatable. Doctors must be honest with these patients. Though it may be difficult to advise someone that they will pass away, it is the correct thing to do. It can allow the patient the opportunity to talk with family and friends, to get his or her personal and financial affairs in order, and to generally make peace. It is possible that the FBI is in its own dying time right now. Perhaps we have gone so far along this incorrect terrorist route that we are irretrievable as a criminal investigative agency. Personally, I believe we are not yet at the FBI's dying time, but we are getting closer. If radical steps are not taken quickly, the FBI may soon be not merely a cancer-racked body but a cancer victim six feet under.

Employees in the FBI (and citizens outside the organization) are in a unique position to right the FBI ship. In cancer, as one enters, or nears, the dying time, one becomes more driven and clearer of spirit and purpose. As this happens in the FBI, perhaps our clarity and drive will allow us to identify a means to save the FBI from its self-induced destruction. It is also possible that with even greater clarity, the organization may still rush headlong into self-destruction. Many agents feel we will no longer be the FBI but, instead, a terrorism watchdog agency more like an organization akin to the Environmental Protection Agency (EPA), which monitors toxic waste. I hope the FBI does not die, but if it occurs, we must hope that the tearing down of our building is at least a step on the road to designing a better antiterrorism agency. Hopefully, we do not need to destroy the entire agency to rebuild a new and functional one. But if this is what must be done, this is what we must do.

Being tough in difficult times has always been the linchpin to bureau success. While we must always obey our FBI managers' work orders, the rank and file need not espouse the same misguided party line. Repeatedly advising management of foolhardy ways may lead to a returned balance between terrorism and criminal work. If you are in the FBI and you continue to be road blocked on criminal cases, push upstream like the salmon. As G. Gordon Liddy put it, "That which does not kill me makes me stronger."

That quotation seems particularly appropriate to current FBI problems and to those with cancer. We cannot get better Thursday unless we make it through Wednesday. Hopefully, by Wednesday, the FBI may realize that only emphasizing terrorism is a dead-end road. I know I will tell everyone who will listen to me that directing the FBI solely toward terrorism is destruction guaranteed.

CHAPTER 9

Miscellaneous Areas Where the FBI Could Improve

This chapter is designed to address individual areas where the FBI could stand improvement but which do not fall under a specific category such as management, OPR, or EEO. In this chapter, I will identify the problem or difficulty and then propose potential solutions in the same subsection of the chapter. However, as I have stated throughout this book, I do not have the market cornered on correct answers. If you identify alternative and superior solutions to these miscellaneous problems, definitely advise the FBI. The bureau can always utilize our citizenry's assistance to help resolve our problems and inadequacies. Here are some varied issues the FBI continues to face.

THE FBI OFTEN MISMANAGES FINANCIAL MATTERS AND SPENDS EXORBITANT AMOUNTS ON RIDICULOUS THINGS BUT WILL NOT EXPEND RELATIVELY MEAGER AMOUNTS ON LEGITIMATE MATTERS

I am sure that in many organizations, both public and private, large and small, financial waste and excess occur. My experience with the FBI makes me conclude that the bureau wastes millions of dollars per year. Additionally, sometimes extremely legitimate requests for funds are denied because of narrow-mindedness and over caution. The FBI's current procedures for approving routine expenditures are cumbersome: ASAC-level approval is required even for minor expenditures such as a one- or two-day covert rental vehicle. Any expense over $2,000 usually requires SAC and/or HQ's approval. Additionally, the government is loath to purchase items, and as a result, items like furniture are rented for years at a time, costing tens of thousands of dollars when purchasing the items would cost much less. Attempting to detail the FBI's ineptitude in the financial arena could take an entire book, but here I will only cover one brief snippet and offer a broad-based solution.

The FBI handles many of its monetary issues haphazardly and with limited overall consistency. The FBI expends money on essential things, necessary things, useful things, wasteful things, and downright stupid things. Conversely, it often is scared and refuses to pay for things that might help solve a case.

The solution is to have a small group of people review any expenditures over a certain dollar amount (say $1,000) to determine legitimacy. To have the same people do all reviews is essential because it provides consistency. The SAC could have final review and approval.

The key, as always, is to err on the side of aggressiveness in investigative matters. If a case agent believes he or she needs to lease a $20,000 apartment to conduct surveillance, this would offer more investigative upside than buying $20,000 of new equipment for the office gym. Financial purchases are broken into various categories and require different approval levels. I am not an expert in the process, but clearly, an outside review should take place so the process can be streamlined and made more efficient and to ensure case-related items receive the appropriate priority they deserve.

Another issue with purchases is that sometimes the riskier large expenses offer the greatest potential investigative awards. In cancer, some types of in-hospital chemotherapy, such as interluken-2, are unbelievably costly with a low likelihood of success. However, when the procedure is successful, 10 percent of patients are completely cured. Even though the absolute percentage may be low, a chance of a complete remission and perfect health for years to come can easily justify the cost of the procedure.

Consider the following. Assume that prior to 9/11, a source reports to the FBI that he is attending an Islamic mosque in Arizona where a number of the members are engaging in fiery rhetoric against the United States. Further, he offers to set up a business in Arizona where these individuals could meet and discuss their dislike for the United States and potentially any disruptive plans they might be hatching. However, the source would need approximately $20,000 to $30,000 to initiate the business. This is an expensive endeavor, which would be very unlikely to have disclosed any of the details of the planning of the 9/11 attacks. Still, a number of the hijackers of the Pentagon plane were, in fact, attending the Tempe, Arizona, mosque prior to the attacks. If we initiated that undercover business, would we have known of the 9/11 plans? It is very unlikely, yet here is an instance where even if a one-in-one-thousand chance existed, the expenditure of the government's money would have been well justified.

The FBI must always walk a difficult line between being frugal in general but potentially financially extravagant when justified by a particular result. Often, financial case-related risk/reward scenarios are very difficult and complex, and this is an area where I possess great empathy for our management. They must make difficult decisions repeatedly. I only offer the suggestion that they try to err on the side of investigative aggressiveness rather than financial micromanagement.

A FEW AGENTS FAIL TO REALIZE THEY ARE PART OF WHAT SHOULD GENERALLY BE A UNIFIED FRONT, AND EVERY SINGLE ONE SHOULD BE A MEMBER OF THE SPECIAL AGENTS ASSOCIATION

Any FBI agent, current or former, reading this book needs to heed my advice in this subsection. The FBI Agents Association (FBIAA) is the only unified voice agents have to speak to Congress, to address the director, and to push forward issues of general relevance to FBI agents.

FBIAA also has a law firm on retainer to assist agents if they become subject to criminal inquiries based on an investigative issue or shooting incident. I do not agree with every position the FBIAA takes, but I always pay my dues and donate other money to it because the association may be an employee's final line of defense in a critical situation, such as a civil lawsuit or criminal charge. If you are an agent and not a member of FBIAA, you should immediately join, and if you do not join, you should be embarrassed to indicate you are part of the brotherhood of the FBI.

When I found out the advanced stage of my brain cancer, one of the first things I vowed to accomplish was to raise money to donate to the Barrow Neurological Institute in Phoenix to help others via research and treatment when the victim was unable to pay for the treatments. I had a retirement party, provided all the attendees a copy of my first book, prizes, and food, and from the money, donated to the institute. It was fantastic that even in a time of great despair myself, I might be able to help someone with similar problems. The

FBIAA is one vehicle FBI employees have to help their fellow workers. Join at the minimum and consider giving the FBIAA additional separate donations.

Always help people in their times of need, even if you are in need as well. Donations to the needy and the downtrodden are worthy endeavors. This is so regardless of your faith system. When I was diagnosed with cancer, many said they would pray for me, and while my own faith system is different, I appreciated everyone's caring thoughts. I myself believe God is within us and all around us in this natural world. Charity is an external manifestation of God's good will.

> Blessed is he who carries within himself
> a god,
> an ideal,
> and who obeys it.
> —Louis Pasteur

For the agents out there, the FBIAA is a nongovernmental organization exclusively for special agents of the FBI: POB 250, New Rochelle, New York, 10801; telephone: (914) 235-8235; e-mail: *FBIAA@compuserve.com*; website: *www.FBIAA.org*.

THE FBI NO LONGER INCORPORATES EMPLOYEES' FAMILIES SUFFICIENTLY INTO THE FBI FOLD

When I entered the bureau over twenty years ago, the organization was much smaller and had the feeling of a family. Due to a change in employee outlook and an increased number of "me generation" employees, we are rapidly losing this family concept. Spouses (and significant others) were immediately taken to dinner or invited to the homes of coworkers and management. If you were single and alone on a holiday, such as Thanksgiving, you would be invited to several homes for football and turkey. Current FBI employees must strive to continue this concept of family. An employee's actual family is his or her primary support system in times of difficulty, and a cancer victim draws enormous emotional strength from family. It is the families in actuality that may be the determining factor in a patient's will to fight and survive. The FBI must similarly support each employee's family by ensuring they realize that when Agent Smith is not able to be home with little Jane and Johnny because of work, any other agent can be immediately made available to assist at Agent Smith's home.

WHEN CONSIDERING UNDERTAKING AN INVESTIGATION, THE FBI SHOULD COMPLETE A PRELIMINARY RISK/REWARD ANALYSIS

The FBI must never fear failure, but we should attempt to ensure that the benefits of potential investigative success are worth the risk of failure. Periodically, white-collar crime (WCC) squads conduct investigations, utilizing thousands of agent man-hours and huge expenditures of government funds, yet even if convicted, the criminal may receive only a nine-month criminal sentence. However, the WCC agents indicate that the deterrent is not the jail time but the loss of the perpetrator's financial or executive position. I am not making a conclusive statement either way, but I do suggest that each case should be weighed on the preliminary scale of justice before significant resources are involved.

It is essential to remember that, periodically, a low likelihood of success is justified. For instance, if the violation is child molestation or a juvenile homicide, FBI personnel expend all efforts. This effort must be put forth even if there is a decidedly low likelihood of success. The risk return in investigations is similar to the issue cancer patients weigh when selecting treatment. Then once a decision is reached, the patient must confidently go forward no matter how significant the potential side effects or danger to life. This is a point where the patient must roll the dice and let the chips fall where they may. Do not second-guess yourself afterward. When the doctors conducted my brain surgery, the best-case scenario was that all my tumors would be gone. The worst-case scenario was that perhaps they would be unable to excise all the tumors, and I might suffer partial paralysis or mental incapacity. In prostate cancer surgery, removal of the prostate might lead to a complete cure, but with the side effects of impotence and incontinence. Deciding which option to take is not an easy decision, but just as in the FBI, make an informed, educated call and then stand by it. After you complete an analysis of the likely outcome, be brave and hold on to your conviction.

ALL AGENTS ARE NOT INTERCHANGEABLE, AND THE POTENTIAL FOR SUCCESS IS INCREASED WHEN THE APPROPRIATE PERSON FOR EACH POSITION IS SELECTED

For virtually all businesses in the world, the leaders and managers of the business attempt to select the most suitable employees for each particular job.

The perfect match does not always occur, but at least an effort is made. In the FBI, a counterintuitive policy has been developed, with the presumption that any agent is fully capable of completing any task. Also, any agent is assumed to be at least minimally qualified to be actually assigned any case as their own. In practice, the FBI is rarely stupid enough to assign newer or unqualified agents to an important investigative matter, but it is not forbidden anymore and is happening more frequently. Everyone should want to be challenged to the fullest extent of his or her abilities, but it is presumptuous to believe that new employees or those working in a new skill area will be able to do more than absorb experienced employees' knowledge. After a sufficient period of exposure and learning, it will then, and only then, be his or her time. If I need a cancer doctor to treat me, I select one familiar with that region of the body or that type of cancer. In a similar vein, agents develop expertise in specific types of investigations. First, new employees should learn how the FBI operates, initially at Quantico, and then via a squad rotational tour in their first field office. Then, based on skills and interest, they should be placed on a permanent squad. This is similar to how doctors are taught. First, the basic skills about anatomy and how systems, such as the central nervous system, operate are explored. Then later, more advanced students specialize in certain areas, like brain cancer, epilepsy, etc.

After agents have a background in the overall methods used in investigations, they should begin to specialize. Often, this specialization will be based on experience both outside and inside the bureau. Someone with a computer background may be selected for the CART (Computer Analysis Recovery Team), or an Arabic language specialist sent to a terrorism squad, and so on. Then after years of remaining on this squad, the agent will build up a true skill base and area (or subarea) of expertise.

One place where the FBI repeatedly butchers this simple concept of beginning with a wide base and then gradually narrowing into areas of skill is with FBI management. The FBI hierarchy believes that once endowed with the label of supervisor (or above), you are now capable of supervising anyone because it is a "people and skills" job, not an experience-curve responsibility. This ugly stick beats us, in the mere agent ranks, throughout our careers. An agent from a white-collar squad in the field is promoted to an FBIHQ supervisor position, which addresses WMD (weapons of mass destruction—think bombs or ricin gas), then is subsequently sent back to the field as a supervisor handling a VCMO squad, which handles kidnappings, fugitives, and violent crimes. These are not interchangeable skills. The WMD supervisor position requires decidedly different skills than a white-collar or drug manager.

One specific area of FBI work with which I am very familiar is undercover agent (UCA) work. During my time in the FBI, I have spent fifteen years in some type of UC role, sometimes full-time undercover, other times of limited duration or depth. I loved my time UC; it was diverse and challenging, and each new role required me to expand my knowledge base and interact with interesting (though frequently violent and strange) new people. There are no experts in UC work, but I feel I had a decent knowledge base, and periodically, other agents felt sufficient confidence in me to ask me questions concerning their own covert investigations. If I did not know the answers, I'd research and contact other UCAs around the FBI (or in other branches of law enforcement) for ideas. I am honored, even now, when an agent asks me a question. I feel that if I can help even in the tiniest way, my experience continues forward in the organization.

While I discuss UCAs, I must make a few additional comments. The FBI loves to hide its UCAs from public sight until their specific skills are needed. Relatively few in management believe UCAs are anything more than potential trouble. You may be brought in to work like a dog for weeks at a time, requested to attempt risky deals, and then when successfully completed, management claims the results and orders you to disappear. In absolutely no way do I suggest all superiors have this mind-set. In fact, any manager (from supervisor to SAC) who has actually completed a difficult longer-term UC role understands the difficulty and the pressure it can place on an agent's family. UCA work is correctly understood by capable UCAs as just one of many potential tools in any investigation, no different from a wiretap, surveillance, or search. The technique does have advantages when executed correctly because you have a credible special agent of the FBI dealing with the actual criminals who can later testify. Additionally, UCAs tend to be inventive and risk takers. While many UCAs are not perfect, and quite a few are a little strange (I definitely am), they are outside the traditional scheme of thinking, yet it can be exactly what an investigation requires.

> The way of a superior man is threefold:
> Virtuous, he is free from anxieties;
> Wise, he is free from perplexities;
> Bold, he is free from fear.
> —*Confucius*

UCAs are not ideal models for all agents, but in some areas, they are extraordinarily good fits. UCAs also are stranger than the general agent group at large, but rarely are they nutcases. The FBI should draw on the expertise of this group more, and it will determine some are even equitable to the superior man Confucius describes.

THE CITIZENS' ACADEMY MAY BE A WASTE OF GOVERNMENT MONEY

The Citizens' Academy is an entity in many larger field offices where prominent citizens are invited to the FBI office and, over a series of weeks, instructed on how the FBI functions. The students are almost exclusively wealthy businessmen or independently well-heeled citizens; attendees pay a fee to attend the instruction, which defers the costs. I personally find the Citizens' Academy a self-serving waste of time. The people attending are generally pro-FBI, so we are not swaying critics to our side. However, the Citizens' Academy does allow management to interact with these businessmen, which heightens the likelihood that one of those well-off businessmen just might hire a retiring FBI supervisor.

I only touch on the Citizens' Academy because I believe the public should know we offer it. Each FBI field office can be contacted to obtain parameters for application. If you are critical of how the FBI operates and you have criticisms, it is you, I hope, who enters the next class. That may help balance out the traditional "love fest." I take care here to specifically note that my opinion is in the minority. While I believe the Citizens' Academy is wasteful, a slight majority of FBI personnel probably believe it to be a positive for the organization.

AGENTS ARE BEGINNING TO LOSE SOME OF THEIR ABILITY TO DEVELOP CONFIDENTIAL INFORMANTS

Confidential informants, or CIs, are the information providers who often create the initial impetus for investigations to begin and continue forward. Developing and maintaining sources takes hard work, intuition, and patience. There are dozens of ideas about how to find sources. Mostly, it just takes experience, effort, and luck. If you are an agent, I offer you three simple suggestions:

1. Find someone on your squad who has multiple quality sources. Ask if you can help with these sources, keep your eyes and ears open, and learn. After a few months, ask that agent if he or she is aware of anyone else who might be a good source. Many senior agents have sources they would be willing to turn over to a competent coworker because they do not have enough time to work all of them.

2. Get away from your damned computer screen. No agent ever found a source logged onto FBINET. Get in your car and go look for someone.

3. Ask your current CIs (or someone else's current CIs) if they are aware of someone else who might like to work for the FBI. The original CI is, by definition, running in the circles you as the agent are interested in. I always offered to pay the original source a finder's fee if it worked out.

ALL FBI EMPLOYEES MUST EMPHASIZE LONG-TERM SUCCESS AND NOT SHORT-TERM QUICK HITS

True success is never short-term, and time horizons for FBI work should be extended. Often, agents become discouraged because an investigation does not proceed quickly enough. Yet it can be the small investigative nuggets gleaned from an unsuccessful case that initiate a successful case years down the road. An interview of a terrorist associate ten years ago might include one single small fact that links a subject to a current criminal incident. This creates an absolute necessity for agents to be detail oriented and specific in their writings. If an FBI employee contemplates broadly and long term, more investigative doors may be able to be opened later. This is a primary reason agents must be doggedly persistent and stubborn when pushing against investigative obstacles. The one goal you are striving toward may in fact be different from the subsequent important achievement that occurs. Though not religious in the traditional sense, I am reminded of the story about how to PUSH and its importance. For those involved with traditional religious ideology, consider the following (also consider how applicable it is to someone fighting cancer):

A man was sleeping one night in his cabin when suddenly his room filled with light, and God appeared. The Lord told the man he had work for him to do and showed him a large rock in front of his cabin. The Lord explained that the man was to push against the rock with all his might. So this the man did, day after day. For many years, he toiled from sun up to sun down, his shoulders set squarely against the cold, massive surface of the unmoving rock, pushing with all his might. Each night, the man returned to his cabin sore and worn out, feeling that his whole day had been spent in vain.

Since the man was showing discouragement, the adversary (Satan) decided to enter the picture by placing thoughts into the weary mind: "You have been pushing against that rock for a long time, and it hasn't moved." Thus, he gave the man the impression that the task was impossible and that he was a failure. These thoughts discouraged and disheartened the man. Satan said, "Why kill yourself over this? Just put in your time, giving just the minimum effort, and that will be good enough." That's what the weary man planned to do but decided to make it a matter of prayer and to take his troubled thoughts to the Lord.

"Lord," he said, "I have labored long and hard in your service, putting all my strength to do that which you have asked. Yet after all this time, I have not even budged that rock by half a millimeter. What is wrong? Why am I failing?"

The Lord responded compassionately, "My friend, when I asked you to serve me and you accepted, I told you that your task was to push against the rock with all your strength, which you have done. Never once did I mention to you that I expected you to move it. Your task was to push. And now as you come to me, your arms are strong and muscled, your back sinewy and brown, your hands are calloused from constant pressure, your legs have become massive and hard. Through opposition, you have grown much, and your abilities now surpass that which you used to have. True, you haven't moved the rock. But your calling was to be obedient and to push and to exercise your faith and trust in my wisdom. That you have done. Now I, my friend, will move the rock."

At times, when we hear a word from God, we tend to use our own intellect to decipher what he wants when actually what God wants is just a simple obedience and faith in him. By all means, exercise the faith that moves mountains but know that it is still God who moves the mountains.

> When everything seems to go wrong . . . just PUSH!
> When the job gets you down . . . just PUSH!
> When people don't react the way you think
> they should . . . just PUSH!

> When your money is "gone" and
> the bills are due ... just PUSH!
> When people just don't understand you ... just PUSH!
> P = Pray
> U = Until
> S = Something
> H = Happens

WE AS FBI AGENTS DO NOT TREAT OUR PROFESSIONAL SUPPORT EMPLOYEES AS WELL AS WE SHOULD

The professional non-agent ranks of the FBI are the backbone of the organization. Often, agents and management are too self-involved to realize that this is where most of the real work is accomplished. These folks who do not often enough receive the credit are the oil and gears that allow this creaky FBI machine to function. I found this true in the medical community as well. While my doctors were great, the hospital nurses, technicians, and support staff were superlative. Anything I asked for while in the hospital from these employees was handled virtually instantaneously. The FBI agent staff could learn important lessons from how doctors courteously treated nurses and technicians. Theirs was more of a team concept than FBI agent/support. Remember one thing that the FBI has in common with the medical profession: our similar missions are to help mankind. Perhaps instead of a Citizens' Academy, we could require all employees to volunteer as hospital support staff for a week.

IF YOU START TO FEEL SORRY FOR YOURSELF IN THE FBI AND BEGIN TO DECREASE YOUR EFFORTS, LEAVE

The FBI is a wonderful job and one in which you periodically actually do some good. There are thousands of qualified people to replace you if you leave the bureau. Never drag the organization down to an individual employee's level of minimized effort. Trust me, whatever slings and arrows of outrageous misfortune you are experiencing in the FBI, they are a drop in the pail compared to a cancer patient's woes. Was it unfair for me to get cancer in my chest and brain? I ate healthy, never smoked, and took care of my physical being. Yes, it was unfair. So what? Other people have even worse things happen. FBI employees have it pretty good. They have an opportunity to help their country and get paid at the same time, so do not ever complain about how bad you have it. If you want out, everyone in your FBI office can show you where the door is. As I say, better dead than deadweight.

CONCLUSION

The best solutions are there with everyone both inside and outside the bureau. Let the organization hear your innovative thoughts. Never weaken in your resolve to be successful. When diagnosed with cancer, you never weaken and give up. Make them take you from the world, kicking and fighting. Remember:

> Defeat is worse than death,
> because you have to
> live with defeat.
> —*Bill Musselman*

CHAPTER 10

Conclusions

Both as a human being and as an FBI agent, I have never been a big fan of conclusions. What may seem like an ending to one individual is merely a beginning for someone else. Some agents incorrectly believe that when their target is finally indicted, arrested, or convicted, their job is completed. Agents more in tune to the longer view realize one arrest is only a link in a very long chain. After being incarcerated, does the agent follow up to determine if the subject may now want to cooperate? Does the inmate continue to operate a criminal enterprise while in custody? Upon eventual release, is the former prisoner likely to return to his criminal ways? It is essential that each FBI employee learn from every case and every interaction with both criminals and non-criminals alike.

> Just remember the world is not a playground
> but a school room.
> Life is not a holiday but an education.
> —*Barbara Jordan*

Cancer patients who want to survive must research all possible types of treatment and therapy and select the option best suited for them. Successful patients, such as those who go into remission or survive longest, generally are handling their lives holistically; they are not merely focusing on the cancer. Instead, they are continuing to live their lives, and while battling the cancer, they are nurturing themselves physically, mentally, and spiritually. In much the same way, the FBI is most successful when it diversifies its efforts and does not foolishly focus on only one area, such as terrorism. The diversity and broad spectrum of knowledge and experience FBI employees possess is the organization's greatest strength. Currently, the FBI is being molded into little more than a domestic antiterrorism entity. This is a grave mistake that could lead to the disintegration of the entire agency or, at a minimum, a degradation of the quality of work performed.

Hopefully, you have found the contents of this book informative or, at least, thought provoking. I believe the juxtaposition of cancer issues with the problems in the bureau is conceptually intriguing. As I endure my treatments for cancer, it deepens my interest in the bureau. It became evident to me that to be successful in my fight against cancer, I would be forced to struggle harder, stay healthier, and maintain a positive mental outlook. For the FBI to survive, it must refocus on its core mission to ensure the protection of American citizens in the broadest sense. The FBI's duty is to protect America from the most dangerous criminals, and the most formidable criminal entities are clearly not limited to terrorists. This narrowing of scope may well hasten the FBI's headlong run into self-destruction. If the FBI emphasizes domestic security only and fails to expeditiously resolve the failings I have identified in this book, the agency will be dismantled or destroyed in relatively short order. I do not personally believe destroying the FBI is the correct response, but as with cancer, there are many resolutions significantly worse than dying. A significant percentage of people stricken with cancer die painful, miserable deaths. If I have a choice, I will fight with all my energy, but if all is eventually lost, then death with dignity is most important.

If the FBI is to endure its own destruction by focusing its work on terrorism only, then the FBI should attempt to pass away with some dignity as well. If the FBI must forego its appropriate mission as a multifaceted agency, then it should die. The hallowed and respected letters *FBI* should never be ascribed to merely a terrorism watchdog group. Splitting the agency apart is much more palatable than falsely indicating to the American citizenry that we continue to be a true federal investigative agency if we are only dealing with terrorists.

Perhaps it is possible that a new director can correct the mistakes and deficiencies inherent in the bureau's current operations. Somewhere, I heard the concept of Ockham's razor, "Pluralitas non est ponenda sine neccesitate," which translates as "Entities should not be multiplied unnecessarily." The easier solution for the FBI is to internally repair its problems concerning management, OPR, bureaucracy, etc., and then settle back and develop a game plan where we continue to fight federal crimes on multiple fronts. This is what the FBI has done for one hundred years: be flexible but stay attuned to our broad overall mission. We should not be so overly focused on one issue that we lose sight of our other responsibilities. When faced with a diagnosis of cancer, the patient must continue to have the faith that he or she will be able to recover. Currently, the FBI is blindly adhering to the narrow terrorism route and is merely getting better at being sick. The FBI is no more effective at fighting terrorism now than prior to 9/11, yet the cost of this major improvement has decimated the organization in all other investigative areas. We may now be more likely to be successful identifying a terrorist entity, but hundreds of additional bank robberies, drug deals, and homicides will go uninvestigated. Hopefully, the changes made since 9/11 have not irretrievably destroyed the FBI's ability to function.

I authored this book believing it was still possible, with input from the public, to pressure the FBI to mend itself. I still have faith. I continue to have faith that I can beat cancer, and I believe I can still impact the FBI for positive change. Faith is a frequently debated, complex, and overwhelming concept. Faith can be religious, nonpartisan, or even both. As I fight with cancer, I am honored and humbled that so many friends, coworkers, and family support me in this time of great need.

If you are ever offered the opportunity to assist the FBI by identifying a new methodology to fight crime or terrorism, I encourage you to help. Tell the FBI your innovative idea. Then tell the bureau again and again. While the agency itself is dysfunctional and narrow minded, specific employees are often spectacular and individually capable of fighting the organization's ingrained stupidity. Even though I have left the FBI for my disability retirement, the bureau will always be able to call me, and I will provide whatever assistance I can.

When I was first diagnosed with cancer, I had everyone pulling for me, and all the faiths were represented. My former girlfriend from my Catholic neighborhood sent me a wonderful card and said she would pray for me. My close Mormon friend from the FBI gave me a CD and said she would pray for me. My godmother who is Lutheran told me she would pray. My ex-wife who claims to be Wiccan (though I think she is Baptist) said she would put in a good word. Even her daughter, who claims to be "down with the devil," said she would help. Since I am an Eastern religion/Zen type, I may in fact have had most of the major faiths covered. To everyone who prayed, wished, or had me in his or her thoughts, I deeply thank you. Now, I would ask that you focus your considerable energies on identifying ideas to help fix the FBI. Then, pass that idea on to the nearest FBI employee you can find. The bureau needs help, and they need it soon. I have faith someone in the public possesses sufficiently innovative ideas that could be utilized to change the FBI and save it from self-destruction.

Be healthy, keep an open mind, and thanks.

> Man's problem in the last analysis
> is man himself.
> A man beset by evil within
> and from without
> can mobilize his spiritual resources
> to conquer that evil.
> Just so can the human race
> mobilize its moral and spiritual power to defeat
> the material power of evil
> that threatens it.
> —Robert E. Byrd

Acknowledgments

Every author experiences a unique type of thrill. It is a thrill of exploration, discovery, and accomplishment. No author would be able to experience any of these emotions were it not for the efforts of dozens of people who assisted behind the scenes.

In my own case, beyond all those who helped with the book, I thank all the doctors, nurses, and support staff of St. Joseph's Hospital, Barrow Neurological Institute, and the Mayo Clinic, who kept me alive after my seizures. My heartfelt love and gratitude is given to my own parents, Al and Marcie Donner, who have always been so supportive and wonderful to me throughout my entire life. My father passed away, but he read a draft copy of this book and made valuable suggestions concerning content, which I incorporated into the book. Dad, I miss you.

I would like to thank all the FBI employees who continue to fight the hard fight against the evil that continues to permeate our society. In particular, I would thank the specific agents who reviewed the draft copies of this book and ensured accuracy and provided suggestions: Gil, Jody, Scott, Mike, Jill, Ken, Brian, and Keith.

It is with great gratitude that I wish to thank Peter and Phyllis Strupp for the knowledge they shared concerning text and publication avenues.

I acknowledge also that I was fortunate to be able to include in this book a number of quotations I believe are representative of the themes I am attempting to convey. A great many of these quotations I located in a book issued by *Forbes* magazine entitled *Thoughts on Virtue*. If you have the opportunity to review this *Forbes* subscriber edition work, you will find the quotes inspiring and thought provoking.

As I completed this book, a fellow agent and friend, Jay Harrison, died after his own battle with melanoma, the same cancer I have. His passing was a terrible loss to his wife, Susan Via, as well as his family and friends. He will be missed.

Finally, I would like to identify by name some of the specific doctors who continue to provide care and kindness to me. Hopefully, I remembered everyone. My undying (perhaps poor terminology) gratitude is extended to the following doctors:

Dr. Kris Smith
Dr. Lynn Ashby
Dr. David Brachman
Dr. Lee Cranmer
Dr. Jay Giancola
Dr. Howard J. Luber
Dr. Royal Anspach
Dr. Jeffrey Isaacs

Appendix I
A Brief History of the FBI

To somewhat butcher a well-known adage:

> Those who do not understand and learn from the ways of the past are doomed to repeat history's mistakes and failures.

Learning the history of the FBI is akin to educating yourself about the disease of cancer. You work better and more effectively in an organization if you understand its historical context, and you can more effectively battle cancer if you understand how cancer grows and destroys.

Founded in 1908, the FBI has a long and storied yet convoluted and twisting history. Any book that attempted to question the operation of the FBI would be remiss not to consider the FBI in an appropriate historical context. One of the weaknesses of many new agents today is that they are not familiar with the basic history of their own organization. Recently, I overheard a group of newly hired agents unable to identify former bureau directors. After hearing the agents' difficulty in naming the directors, I stepped in and identified their names (including those of most of the acting directors).

Following this, a female agent responded, "Why should I care about Hoover? He never allowed female agents, and he was the one who wore a dress!"

Humorous no doubt, but this agent was wrong. J. Edgar Hoover, however he was attired in private (and no one, absolutely no one, has ever confirmed him owning skirts), is the most important individual in the history of law enforcement.

Bureau of Investigation (BI) Directors (1907-1935)

#	Picture	Name	Period
1		Stanley Finch	July 26, 1908 – April 30, 1912
2		A. Bruce Bielaski	April 30, 1912 – February 10, 1919
—		William E. Allen	February 10, 1919 – June 30, 1919
3		William J. Flynn	July 1, 1919 – August 21, 1921
4		William J. Burns	August 22, 1921 – May 10, 1924
5		J. Edgar Hoover	May 10, 1924 – June 30, 1935

Federal Bureau of Investigation (FBI) Directors (1935–present)

#	Picture	Name	Period	Length
1		J. Edgar Hoover	July 1, 1935 – May 2, 1972	36 years, 10 months
—		L. Patrick Gray	May 3, 1972 – April 27, 1973	Acting (11 months)
—		William Ruckelshaus	April 30, 1973 – July 9, 1973	Acting (3 months)

Appendix I / 131

2		Clarence M. Kelley	July 9, 1973 – February 15, 1978	4 years, 6 months
—		James B. Adams	February 15, 1978 – February 23, 1978	Acting (8 Days)
3		William H. Webster	February 23, 1978 – May 25, 1987	9 years, 3 months
—		John E. Otto	May 26, 1987 – November 2, 1987	Acting (7 months)
4		William S. Sessions	November 2, 1987 – July 19, 1993	6 years, 8 months
—		Floyd I. Clarke	July 19, 1993 – September 1, 1993	Acting (2 months)
5		Louis Freeh	September 1, 1993 – June 25, 2001	7 years, 9 months
—		Thomas J. Pickard	June 25, 2001 – September 4, 2001	Acting (3 months)
6		Robert Mueller	September 4, 2001 – Present	11 years, 3 months and 1 day

As a side note, *The Investigator* published an article in May 1981, reporting that while the two women who entered the FBI in July 1972 were often regarded as the first female FBI agents, this was not technically true. When Hoover took over the organization in 1924, there were actually two female agents already on duty, and Lenore Houston, appointed in 1924, worked within the agency until 1928. It was J. Edgar Hoover who authorized the designation of Houston as an agent in November 1924.

The concept of the previous story is not to suggest that Hoover was an open-minded champion of female rights. The reason there were no female agents between 1928 and Hoover's death in 1972 is directly related to Hoover himself and to the historical context of women's oppression during that period. Still, unless you know your facts, it is probably better to remain silent. If more FBI employees learned the history of the organization, they would be more humble and understand they are a small piece of a massive historical dynamic. The FBI, while made up of human flesh, is much more than any one employee.

The history of the FBI can be a tremendously enlightening vehicle to understand why the FBI has huge strengths and similarly massive weaknesses. While much of this book criticizes aspects of the organization, I respect its history. Much of my criticism will hopefully come with suggestions for correction. Still, as I requested in my introduction, I do not possess all, or even most, of the answers. I need your help to repair an organization, which, while fundamentally flawed, is fixable.

To provide legitimate critique, detractors and reconstructionists alike must know the FBI's background. The strength of an organization is its flexibility in a time of crisis, and its weakness is rigidity to change. When you are assessing the history, observe where rigidity was a downfall and, when thinking outside the box, where it created astounding triumphs. There are many books that offer either an abridged version of the bureau's entire history or relate a full-blown tale of some particular case or career. Some of these books are good, some bad, and many self-serving. Here are a few I recommend to provide some perspective on the FBI's operations:

The FBI Story by Don Whitehead
Published in 1956, this Hoover-authorized work paints
the "old FBI" in a beautiful patina as almost infallible;
still, it is universally quoted by later authors.

Hoover's FBI by William W. Turner
Originally published in 1970 and subsequently reissued, this book is the antithesis of *The FBI Story*. It is a sometimes scathing criticism of the FBI under J. Edgar Hoover.

The Complete Idiot's Guide to the FBI
by John Simeone and David Jacobs
Published in 2003, this book traces the history of the FBI from inception to the reorganization after the terrorist acts of September 11, 2001. If you want facts, this is the book.

The Bureau by Ronald Kessler
Reissued in 2002, this book provides storied tales and humor that are legendary in the FBI and seldom heard outside the organization.

Donnie Brasco by Joseph Pistone
Published in January 1989, this gripping book tells the story of Pistone's penetration into the highest levels of the Mafia in New York City. This is a must-read when considering the FBI as it applies to undercover work. And by the way, if anyone reading this book has my autographed copy of it given to me when I was working deep undercover, return it to me!

Mobbed Up by James Neff
Published in 1989, this detail-oriented book tells of teamster president Jackie Presser's life and relationship with the Mafia and the FBI. It clearly demonstrates the FBI at its best and worst when dealing with confidential informants.

Cold Zero by Christopher Whitcomb
Published in 2001, this spectacularly well-written, though sometimes self-serving, book tells a very complete story of the FBI's Hostage Rescue Team (HRT).

Though these are just a sampling of books about the FBI, they are extremely useful writings. For general background, I would endorse *The Complete Idiot's Guide to the FBI*. The writing provides detailed, concise, chronological, and semi neutral background. Before I begin providing a summarized history of the organization, I thank the authors of the above books for much of the information I co-opted (and hopefully did not plagiarize) to write this historical section. Additionally, I would be remiss if I did not thank the FBI employees who contributed to the FBI's own Internet (and intranet) sites where I found many historical tidbits.

Here is an encapsulated history of the FBI, 1908 to the present, over one hundred years of law enforcement trials, successes, and errors.

The history of the bureau can essentially be divided onto four broad time frames:

The initial years (prior to Hoover being named director in 1924)
The Hoover years (1924 to 1972)
The new FBI (1972 to September 11, 2001)
The FBI since the terrorist acts of 9/11

THE INITIAL YEARS

The FBI, or Bureau of Investigation (BI), was initiated in 1908 by then Attorney General Charles J. Bonaparte when he hired nine investigators and a dozen or so support staff. Initial reports to Congress identified the agency's mission as the enforcement of slavery laws, banking fraud laws, antitrust laws, and laws involving crimes on government reservations.

In 1908, the idea of federal law enforcement was perceived by many as almost totalitarian; most believed law enforcement was best kept at the state and local levels. Regardless of these concerns, the BI gradually acquired more investigative responsibilities and, commensurately, more influence. Two keys to the increasing role of the FBI were individual laws that expanded jurisdiction, and individual societal concerns that increased pressure to conduct higher profile investigations.

In 1910, the Mann Act, or White Slave Traffic Act, made it illegal to transport a woman across state lines for immoral purposes. Immediately, the bureau started working "pimp and prostitute" cases. When war broke out in 1917, the public wanted increased scrutiny of subversives and espionage. After World War I, the Leninists and Reds became the new threat. During much of the 1920s, the BI (and a newly hired underling named J. Edgar Hoover) battled the Red Menace.

Prohibition was the next great law empowering the BI. Mobsters and corruption were the order of the day, and the BI was not immune. After a number of scandals within the agency, Hoover was named director in 1924.

Hoover immediately began to professionalize the BI, which was renamed the Federal Bureau of Investigation in 1934.

THE HOOVER YEARS (1924 TO 1972)

The years of the early 1920s through the mid-1930s were often referred to as the lawless period due to the strength of ethnic (German, Irish, and Italian) organized crime and the general populace's repudiation of prohibition. Prohibition, the so-called noble experiment, was a universal failure, which enabled gangsters to profit and gain public acceptance. Though directly enforcing prohibition violations fell to the Department of the Treasury, the BI often became involved. Most importantly, the bureau began to find ways to obtain jurisdiction by hook or by crook (add emphasis on "crook") when there was a public perception that a group or individual posed a threat. The bureau "manufacturing jurisdiction" is a very proactive way of fighting crime. It is a way to ensure that big fish go to jail. As examples, Al Capone was investigated as a federal witness of interest, and Ku Klux Klan members were investigated as espionage subjects and violators of the Mann Act.

In the early 1920s, despite some successes, the bureau was replete with incompetence and downright corruption. When Hoover took over, he dismissed agents he felt were unqualified and incompetent and set hiring and promotion standards. He established guidelines for investigations and began to regularly inspect field offices; a formal training program was initiated for new hires in the late 1920s. Perhaps the greatest achievement in Hoover's early tenure was development of the Identification Division, which served as a repository for fingerprints taken during law enforcement investigations. By the late 1920s, many local law enforcement agencies began to send fingerprint cards to the bureau. As a result, the massive number of prints became the means to assist investigations by linking crime scene prints to previously identified criminals. This process, though much more refined, continues to be coordinated by the FBI today.

The Wall Street Crash of 1929 brought hard times for all but the gangsters. Outlaws—including John Dillinger, "Pretty Boy" Floyd, Ma and Pa Barker, and "Baby Face" Nelson—ruled the day (and night). In 1933, an event forever changed the FBI when captured bank robber Frank "Jelly" Nash was "freed" by three gunmen in Kansas City. In the Kansas City Massacre, the gunmen killed four law enforcement officers (including Bureau Agent Raymond Caffery). In the melee, Nash was also killed. Based on this incident, a series of federal laws were passed authorizing agents to carry firearms and, more importantly, expanding the bureau's jurisdiction. Jurisdiction was expanded by making the following federal offenses:

- Rob a federally insured bank
- Assault or kill a federal agent
- Flee across state lines to avoid capture
- Transport stolen property across state lines

Additionally, the FBI assumed jurisdiction in kidnapping cases if the victim was missing for more than seven days.

These new federal offenses and the ability to carry weapons and make arrests allowed the FBI to more successfully combat gangsters. It was also during the 1930s that the term "G-man" came into popular usage. G-men (government men) were popularized as criminal super sleuths in comics, magazines, and movies. Hoover quickly saw the value of the publicity and fostered the image.

During the 1930s, whether truth or fiction, the FBI was credited with the capture (or killing) of numerous well-known gangsters:

- George "Machine Gun" Kelly
- Alvin "Creepy" Karpis
- "Baby Face" Nelson
- "Pretty Boy" Floyd
- John Dillinger

Along with great press and successes came two other important developments. The bureau expanded a nascent laboratory section to handle the processing of physical evidence, and the National Academy, begun in 1935, trained local and state police officers in the most modern investigative skills. Today, these two institutions continue to contribute to law enforcement success worldwide.

Soon, the FBI acquired another obligation—to investigate the Nazi and communist threats. With the possible exception of the American Revolution, the time period surrounding World War II was the most important in US history. As the coalition of Italy, Japan, and Germany battled virtually everyone except the United States and Russia, fascism and communism spread to

America. In 1936, the FBI was officially authorized to launch investigations against subversives who sought to overthrow the government.

The FBI successfully exposed American fascist groups, including the German-American Bund and the Liberty League, and covertly worked against communism. Russia had signed a neutrality pact with Germany, but in 1941, Germany attacked Russia. The American-based communists who had advocated neutrality were stunned. On December 7, 1941, the Japanese bombed Pearl Harbor, and America entered the war. The FBI immediately became responsible for draft evasion and sabotage matters.

During the war, the bureau uncovered a plot by the Germans to destroy targets with explosives after dropping personnel off by submarine in New York. The FBI was also responsible for arresting Japanese, Germans, and Italians considered as threats. The war ended in September 1945 on one of the few occasions where good triumphed over evil.

The postwar world presented new challenges for the FBI as communism and espionage became paramount concerns. Persuasive information indicated that procommunist elements had infiltrated US businesses and even the government itself. The FBI determined that a top American government employee named Alger Hiss was a secret Soviet agent. Hiss had previously testified before Congress that he was merely a loyal State Department leader and had nothing but admiration for the United States. Yet Hiss was soon disproved when a former associate in the Communist Party produced writings from a hollowed-out pumpkin (the Pumpkin Papers), which proved Hiss had provided confidential documents to Soviet handlers. In January 1950, Hiss was convicted of perjury regarding his congressional testimony and sentenced to a five-year prison term.

In 1949, the Soviets successfully completed an atomic weapon test, and atomic fear swept through the nation. It was clear that someone within the US nuclear development group had disclosed information from the Manhattan Project to the Soviet Bloc. The FBI was able to prove that a number of Soviet spies had compromised the data, and the following spies were exposed and/or prosecuted:

Dr. Klaus Fuchs
David Greenglass
Harold Gold
Morton Sobell
Joel Barr

Alfred Sarant
William A. Perl
Max Elitcher
Julius Rosenberg
Ethel Rosenberg

Most of these traitors were prosecuted. Two escaped to the Soviet Union (Barr and Sarant), and two were executed (the Rosenbergs).

As the 1950s progressed, the threat of communism diminished in part due to the FBI's surveillance. During the same time that the FBI battled spies and Reds, its jurisdiction on the criminal front continued to expand. Authority to investigate illegal gambling and racketeering allowed the bureau to identify its next target of opportunity, the Mafia.

Prior to the late 1950s, Hoover (and therefore the FBI) had denied the existence of an organized La Cosa Nostra (LCN). This shortsightedness left the FBI years, if not decades, behind in fighting organized crime. Many within the organization clearly were aware of the problem, but until Hoover officially recognized the issue, it did not exist. An event occurred in 1957 that spurred the FBI to officially acknowledge the mob. In Appalachin, New York, most of the leaders of the Mafia met for a little pasta and a lot of planning. When the meeting was interrupted, dozens of mobsters fled and were subsequently stopped and identified. The existence of the Mafia could no longer be denied, and Hoover acknowledged this and began to authorize OC (organized crime) investigations.

Based largely on the urging of newly appointed Attorney General Robert Kennedy, numerous Mafia figures were indicted and convicted. Additionally, mob soldier Joseph Valachi testified before Congress, and the organizational hierarchy of the Mafia was exposed. With the use of wiretaps and undercover agents, by the 1980s, Mafia influence had been reduced.

When discussing the late 1950s and 1960s, it would be remiss not to mention the animosity between Hoover and President John F. Kennedy and his brother, the attorney general. The hatred went deep on both sides. The 1960s were a tumultuous time for the country and the FBI. Many view the 1960s as a time of idealism, racial improvement, and love. History without blinders will more correctly judge the decade as marred by violence, racial strife, and disruptive demonstrations. The FBI responded to these threats (both real and imagined) with new techniques, including wiretaps (both legal and illegal), Cointelpro (counter-informational schemes), and harassment. The scope of this historical section would never permit the space to include a full explanation of the FBI's abuses of constitutional rights that occurred in the 1960s. What can definitely be said about Cointelpro is that it was utilized to harass causes Hoover found abhorrent and was a proactive disruption technique that if used today would land any current agent in jail for civil rights violations. Cointelpro efforts targeted the KKK (all right, I do not find that too terrible), the Black Panthers (I probably do not care much either—except see below*), the radical new left (I care some), and Martin Luther King Jr. (I personally care quite a lot—see particularly below**).

During this time, the FBI both abused its obligation and was an embarrassment to the American public. The bottom line is clear: it was a dirty decade in the organization's history.

There were, however, three things the FBI did not do:

1. The FBI did not conspire to kill either John Kennedy or Robert Kennedy. Hoover knew so much about the brothers that there was no need to have them killed.

2. The FBI was not involved in the killings of either Martin Luther King Jr. or Malcolm X. There are conspiracy buffs who drone endlessly about conspiracies involving the FBI related to the deaths of the Kennedys, Malcolm X, King, and numerous others. Could the CIA be involved? I don't know (ask one of them). Yet I state here that the FBI is too bureaucratic and filled with too many covering-their-asses types to ever be involved in a murder plot. Could an individual agent do it alone? Yes, so long as he kept quiet about it. Regardless, I do not know any agents who have admitted to killing anyone of that stature, though someone like G. Gordon Liddy at least had the moxie.

3. The FBI did not internally deny the existence of drugs or the Mafia. Hoover knew the threat of drugs and the mob but did not want his agents to become involved in these investigations. After Hoover's

---

* After three Black Panthers were killed in gang warfare, an internal FBI memo claimed credit for stirring up the dissension that led to the deaths (how repulsive).

** Hoover began to strongly dislike Martin Luther King Jr. after he openly criticized the FBI. Accordingly, wiretaps of King were authorized, and his sexual and amorous endeavors were highlighted and forwarded to his wife, Coretta King. Additionally, Hoover had a letter sent to MLK, suggesting King commit suicide.

death, the bureau began to actively investigate drugs and organized crime.

FBI Director Hoover (some would say the only "real" director) died on May 2, 1972, after almost fifty years as head of the organization. Hoover had outlived fans, critics, presidents, and all political usurpers. Hoover was the ultimate survivor, and he had converted a ragtag, weaponless bunch of nobodies into the premier law enforcement agency in the world. In my opinion, he is the most important person in law enforcement history. Find him distasteful, deceitful, or even evil, but never deny the influence he wielded.

There have been significant criticisms of J. Edgar Hoover and his tenure as the head of the FBI. Many were unfounded and many well deserved. In my own time in the organization, I have spent a considerable amount of time working against drugs, organized crime, and the Mafia in an undercover role. The Mafia's doctrine of *omerta*, or code of silence, can be interpreted as a sworn oath to never betray the secrets of the crime family. In many ways, the same holds true for the FBI, and while there will be those who claim I am breaking the bureau's code of *omerta*, Hoover never did. He steadfastly lived by a code akin to the Mafia creed later intercepted over an FBI wiretap during a Mafia initiation ceremony in Boston. As one contemplates the following intercepted quotation, consider that Hoover would be proud:

> *I want to enter alive into this organization,*
> *and I will have to get out dead. Only the fucking ghosts*
> *know what really took place here by God.*

Only Hoover (spinning in his grave though he may now be) could honestly and completely relate the history of the FBI prior to 1972. Rest in peace.

THE NEW FBI (1972 TO SEPTEMBER 11, 2001)

Two history-changing events occurred in 1972 that would forever alter the public perception of the FBI. The first was Hoover's death. The second occurred when discovery of the Watergate break-in led to investigations disclosing widespread wrongdoings by the FBI. One of the principal architects of the break-in and other questionable tactics employed by CREEP (Committee to Reelect the President) was former FBI Agent G. Gordon Liddy. Liddy was an unusual figure in his own right, and anyone interested in the man should read his autobiography, *Will*. For all of Liddy's oddities, he truly believed in his causes. I have always personally respected Liddy because of all the people associated with the illegal activities of CREEP, he was the only one stand-up enough not to rat out his coconspirators. For his silence, he was rewarded with an extended jail term in a high-security facility while other more culpable players received light sentences. Regardless of Liddy's former ties to the FBI, it was not his role in Watergate that tarnished the FBI. A much darker secret was looming around the corner.

After Hoover's death, Richard Nixon appointed L. Patrick Gray as acting director. Gray was forced to resign in 1973 after admitting he had destroyed documents found in the safe of a Watergate burglar. After this blow to FBI credibility, former agent and Kansas City police chief Clarence M. Kelley was appointed director to clean up the scandals left by Gray and the abuses of the 1960s.

Director Kelley sought to restore public trust in the FBI by instituting career boards to identify and train management and worked with the Department of Justice to codify guidelines for bureau investigations into foreign counterintelligence. Additionally, Kelley emphasized quality over quantity of cases and diversified the agent population by hiring more women and minorities. In 1978, Kelley resigned and was replaced by former federal judge William H. Webster. Webster, even after his appointment, preferred to be addressed as judge rather than director.

As a brief interlude, I note that Webster was the first director I worked for, and while he did a number of good things for the organization, my only historical comment is that he was no ball of fire as an orator. Just before I was scheduled to graduate from the FBI Academy, the class counselor told us we would be going to headquarters to have a brief meeting with Webster. The counselor advised us to call him judge or sir but not director and added, "Whatever you do, do not fall asleep while the judge is speaking." I laughed inside, thinking how silly it was to even suggest that because we were all so new and eager. We would be hanging on his every word. With hindsight, I may have hung on every word, but I wish I had consumed additional caffeine that morning because by the time I left, I had whiplash from trying not to allow my chin to hit my chest as I fought sleep. A firebrand and rousing speaker like Clarence Darrow our judge was surely not.

Under Webster, the FBI expanded operations into public corruption and successfully prosecuted members of the judiciary (Operation Greylord), Congress (Abscam), and defense contractors (Illwind). The FBI also received concurrent jurisdiction for drug violations and successfully prosecuted major drug cases. To respond to potential terrorist threats, hostage situations, and other complex tactical issues, the FBI also created the elite Hostage Rescue Team (HRT).

During (and after) Webster's tenure, the FBI had remarkable success combating the Mafia. The bureau basically decimated the major crime families, utilizing wiretaps (most obviously the Boston wire that recorded the initiation ceremony), informants (most notably Jackie Presser, president of the Teamsters), and undercover agents (most famously Agent Joe Pistone, a.k.a. Donnie Brasco, who infiltrated the New York Bonnano crime family).

During the 1980s, FBI investigations uncovered high-level government personnel who were spying either for the Soviets, East Germans, or other countries. These spies caused the loss of classified material and undoubtedly cost many people their lives. One theme that runs throughout the FBI's history is its absolutely stunning success combating spies. The success runs from the spies of the 1920s to the FBI's own mole, Robert P. Hanssen, who was exposed only in 2001. In the 1980s alone, the following traitors were identified:

> John A. Walker Jr. (Navy)
> Ronald W. Pelton (NSA)
> Edward Lee Howard (CIA Associate)
> Richard W. Miller (FBI)
> Jonathan J. Pollard (Navy Intelligence)
> Larry Wu-Tai Chin (CIA)

The two most abhorrent spies in history were CIA division head Aldrich Ames and FBI supervisor Robert P. Hanssen. These two turncoat traitors, who were arrested in 1994 (Ames) and 2001 (Hanssen), both spied for the Soviets for more than twenty years. Their actions led to the compromise of numerous investigations and the murders of dozens of counterintelligence operatives. Both cut deals to avoid the death penalty, and without exception, the view inside the FBI agent population is that both should have been executed for their crimes.

In 1987, Judge Webster left the FBI and was named head of the CIA (I am certain the quantity of high-dosage caffeine consumed at CIA headquarters in Langley skyrocketed). To replace Webster as director of the FBI, another former federal judge was named: William Steele Sessions.

Due to the fall of the Iron Curtain and the Berlin Wall, Sessions redirected a significant portion of agents away from national security matters and toward violent crime. The volume of violent crime had increased dramatically in the 1980s, and to combat it, the FBI set up task forces with local and state law enforcement. Additionally, under Sessions, the FBI began to consider the security of business trade secrets and cyber crime.

Steele may not have been the best middle name for Director Sessions. He was a very nice man who took to pinning his FBI badge on his shirt over his heart. He also broke his elbow while he was under scrutiny for ethics violations involving inappropriate items and services received by himself and his wife. Eventually, after he considered barricading himself in his office, he came to his senses and resigned. Former agent, federal prosecutor, and federal judge Louis J. Freeh replaced him in September 1993.

Freeh arrived with a clear agenda. He would streamline FBIHQ and transfer more agents to the streets and would expand the FBI's overseas contingent by expanding the legal attaché (LEGAT) program. Unfortunately for Director Freeh, two events took place that caused both the public and Congress to question the FBI's ability to respond to crisis.

In August 1992, the FBI responded to the shooting death of a deputy US marshal near Ruby Ridge, Idaho. HRT responded, and during the course of the standoff, the main subject's wife was accidentally shot and killed by an HRT sniper. Eight months later, outside of Waco, Texas, HRT watched as members of a religious sect lit themselves on fire at the command of their leader, David Koresh. Eighty people died in the blaze, and the FBI took all the heat.

The bottom line is the FBI often makes mistakes, but in these two incidents, the FBI acted in the appropriate way. The sniper in the Ruby Ridge matter did exactly what he was trained to do. It was Randy Weaver (the suspect in the killing of the US marshal) who put his wife in harm's way. At Waco, no one ever thought it possible a self-lit inferno would erupt. The media crucified the FBI for situations botched at inception by ATF. Regardless of fault, the incidents were public relations disasters made worse when the FBI did not immediately come forward and clearly justify each action that was taken.

Crime changes and is fluid, and so must law enforcement adapt and change as well. Based partly on the media spin on Ruby Ridge and Waco, hate groups had a new cause—the FBI.

Antigovernment groups began, in the 1990s, to grow in strength and visibility. They also proved extremely deadly. Most antigovernment groups are homegrown, but can be international as well. In the 1990s, the FBI investigated such hatemongers with both successes and miscues:

1. UNABOMB—The FBI successfully located Theodore Kaczynski and stopped his eighteen-year reign of terror of sending explosive packages to innocent people.

2. Atlanta Olympic Park Bombing—The FBI harassed and violated the rights of innocent security officer (and actual hero) Richard Jewell. In the Jewell case, the bureau relied too heavily on how closely Jewell fit the profile of a likely bomber.

3. OKBOMB—The FBI diligently and tirelessly went through voluminous evidence and linked Timothy McVeigh to the bombing of the Oklahoma City Federal Building. McVeigh was subsequently executed for his crime. Again, in a public relations disaster, disclosures just prior to the execution made it appear that the FBI withheld evidence. This is a falsehood, and any error in this regard should rest squarely on the narrow shoulders of the Department of Justice attorneys who ridiculously agreed to provide McVeigh's attorneys *all* documents related to the investigation, not merely the documents related to his innocence or guilt. Evidence related directly or indirectly to culpability and innocence is the normal, legitimate standard for discovery. The traditional standard is the only one that should have been used.

4. Wen Ho Lee—The FBI believed Lee had provided nuclear secrets to the People's Republic of China after determining he had made unauthorized copies of nuclear weapon codes. He was indicted and held in solitary confinement prior to trial. The difficulties mounted, however, when the FBI could not prove all the charges, and all but one were subsequently dropped. Yet unlike the Richard Jewell fiasco, Wen Ho Lee was guilty of subterfuge and deception; he may have been a spy as well. The FBI just could not prove it.

5. TRADEBOMB—In 1993, the FBI successfully linked a blind sheik from New Jersey (Omar Abdel Rahman), Ramzi Yousef, and others to

the initial truck bombing at the World Trade Center. Unfortunately, this successful case was just the tip of the FBI's next iceberg.

THE FBI SINCE THE TERRORIST ACTS OF SEPTEMBER 11, 2001

One of the gravest inaccuracies of the mainstream media is that many perceive 9/11 as a seminal terrorist event. It is more appropriately viewed as one step in a horrific continuation of terror. Still, the incidents on September 11 must be viewed as the event that will forever alter how the FBI functions. The current FBI director, Robert S. Mueller III, took office one week before 9/11 and has subsequently shaken the FBI to its very foundation by avowing that the bureau's primary and only true focus will be domestic security. All other matters—drugs, violent crime, white-collar crime, cyber crime, etc.—take a backseat to the FBI's job of protecting domestic security. It may sound good on paper, but in practice, it still remains to be seen. In this book, I have devoted an entire chapter to this issue of Director Mueller's view for the FBI. It is a contentious issue within our organization, and one that many employees are afraid to discuss due to Mueller's steadfast desire for it to be our agency's focus.

Before closing this historical section, I would like to emphasize the power of a terrorist organization like al-Qaeda, headed formerly by Osama bin Laden. Most US citizens deservedly fixate on the 9/11 attacks when thinking of al-Qaeda. Consider the following incidents (all directly linked to al-Qaeda) as merely a timeline of hate. All these incidents were attacks against American citizens either at home or abroad:

1. February 1993—The first World Trade Center bombing (6 killed, hundreds injured).

2. 1996—The Khobar Tower bombing in Dhahran, Saudi Arabia (19 US servicemen killed, dozens severely wounded).

3. August 1998—Truck bombings in Dar Es Salaam, Tanzania, and Nairobi, Kenya (224 people killed, approximately 5,000 injured).

4. December 1999—FBI agents arrest Ahmed Ressam at the Canadian border as he attempted to bring a carload of explosives into the United

States, intending to bomb Los Angeles International Airport (0 killed, 0 wounded, but consider the potential disaster that was averted).

5. October 2000—Navy destroyer USS *Cole* is bombed in Yemen by a small motorboat (17 sailors killed, dozens wounded).

6. September 2001—World Trade Center destroyed (3,000 killed), Pentagon attacked (189 killed), US Capitol targeted by Flight 93 and plane crashes in Pennsylvania (37 killed).

7. June 2002—Car bomb at US Consulate in Karachi (12 killed).

8. October 2002—Bali downtown bombing (202 killed, over 200 injured).

9. May 2003—US residential complexes destroyed by car bombs in Riyadh, Saudi Arabia (26 killed, 160 wounded).

10. October 2003—Bomb detonation at US diplomatic convoy (3 Americans killed).

The numbers of dead and wounded are staggering, and know that there were other plots that were foiled both inside and outside the United States. This is a war on many fronts, and the FBI will be forced to be malleable and change to fight this and all new enemies. The history of the FBI may be just getting started. Now we need to talk about fixing the FBI to create a future more likely to be one of successes against our enemies.

Appendix 2

Set out in full text are instructions on conducting OPR investigations and a letter from the Administrative Services Division (dated October 24, 2003) addressing the use of indefinite suspensions in personnel matters. I have removed from the letter the names of the sending and receiving parties, as well as the file numbers.

Addendum 1

Conducting OPR Investigations:
The following information is being provided to each SAC/Division Head as guidelines for conducting the OPR investigation that is being referred to your division. Questions regarding specifics of the inquiry should be referred to the case supervisor listed on the enclosed EC.

Upon the initiation of an OPR inquiry, the subject of the inquiry should be presented with an OPR Notification Form. This Notification Form will be forwarded from OPR. Upon presentation of the Notification Form, the subject of the OPR is to be advised that at any time he/she can voluntarily submit documentation, information, or other evidence, which he/she wishes to be considered in OPR's resolution of the inquiry.

As the receiving division you are being requested to conduct an OPR investigation into this matter as set forth in the details of the attached EC.

Receiving division is requested to ensure that investigation in this matter is assigned to senior, mature personnel having no direct investigative or performance responsibility with regard to the subject or with witnesses in this inquiry.

Each Division is reminded of the requirement to conduct this inquiry in an expeditious manner. This requirement is based on litigation requiring the timely resolution of administrative internal inquiries conducted regarding allegations of serious misconduct involving FBI employees.

Receiving Division is requested to conduct an OPR investigation regarding the allegation(s) in accordance with MIOG, Part I, Section 263, and the Director's airtels to all ADICs, et al., entitled "Delegations of Disciplinary Action Authorities to ADICs and FBIHQ Division Heads," dated 2/23/94 and 1/30/95. Pursuant to the Director's airtels, this investigation should be completed by BUDED. The results of the investigation should be reported to OPR in the form of a summary EC (original and three copies), in accordance with OPR's EC to All Field Offices and FBIHQ Divisions, dated 1/22/98, and forwarded to OPR, to the attention of the case supervisor on enclosed EC.

Conducting Interviews:

Interviews of Non-FBI employees should be reported utilizing an FD-302.

Interviews of FBI employees must be reported in the form of a typed signed, sworn statement (SSS). At the outset of the interview, the employees must be advised that if they lie during an inquiry, they can expect to be dismissed from the rolls of the FBI.

All interviews should be conducted and witnessed by two senior personnel. The interviewee should initial each page of the SSS. Also, the interviewee should initial the beginning of the text of the SSS and the end of the text of the SSS. The final sentence of the SSS should read, "I have read this statement consisting of this and X other pages and it is true and correct." (The total amount of pages of the SSS, other than the signatory page, should be substituted for the X.)

All interviews of FBI employees must be conducted utilizing one of the following:

1. *Administrative Inquiry:*
   FD-645: Warning and Assurance to Employee Required to Provide Information;

The employee's signed, sworn statement must include, toward the outset, the sentence, "I understand from my review of the FD-645 that should I 'refuse to answer or fail to reply fully and truthfully' during this interview, which I further understand would place me in violation of the Director's 'Bright Line' pronouncement, I can expect to be dismissed from the rolls of the FBI." "The employees" statement should be concluded by stating "have been instructed not to discuss this matter with anyone other than the person(s) conducting this interview, representatives from the OPR

FBIHQ, an FBI Employee Assistance Program (EAP) Counselor, and/or my attorney. I have been told that should I decide to discuss this matter with anyone else, I must first obtain authorization from the interviewer(s)."

2. Criminal Inquiry:
   FD-644: Warning and Assurance to Employee Requested to Provide Information on a Voluntary Basis.

The employee's signed, sworn statement must include, toward the outset, the sentence, "I have been further advised of my rights and responsibilities in connection with this inquiry as set forth on a "Warning and Assurance to Employee Requested to Provide Information on a Voluntary Basis" form FD-644 which I have read and signed. I understand that should I decide to reply and thereafter furnish false information during this interview, I could be found to be in violation of the Director's "Bright Line" pronouncement and can expect to be dismissed from the rolls of the FBI." The employee's statement should be concluded by stating "I have been instructed not to discuss this matter with anyone other than the person(s) conducting this interview, representatives from the OPR, FBIHQ, and FBI Employee Assistance Program (EAP) Counselor, and/or my attorney. I have been told that should I decide to discuss this matter with anyone else, I must first obtain authorization from the interviewer(s)."

In the course of conducting an OPR inquiry, if the subject makes admissions to additional non-criminal misconduct outside of the issued notification, the interview can continue. However, it is stipulated that the subject must be advised prior to further questioning that they will receive a new notification form from the AD, OPR delineating the new allegations. The new notification may result in further investigation and interviews.

If the interviewers determine that the subject is making admissions of criminal activity for misconduct, then this line of questioning cannot be pursued until so authorized by AD, OPR. The scope of the interview must proceed in accordance with the notification or then telephonically followed by EC with the known information and are to conduct no extenuating investigation. In turn, OPR will consult with the Department of Justice, Office of Professional Responsibility (DOJ/OPR) for a prosecuting opinion. Based upon these consultations, OPR will forward the appropriate notification and guidance to the concerned division. This guidance is to ensure compliance with the parameters and spirit of the Director's March 1997 "Bright Line" communication.

An original and three copies of each SSS or FD-302 should be forwarded as enclosures to the summary EC. The original notes supporting each SSS or FD-302 should be placed in an FD-340 (1A Envelope) along with the corresponding FD-644 or FD-645. Any other original documentation should be forwarded to OPR as an enclosure to the summary EC.

Receiving division for captioned subject is requested to provide specific input regarding subject that will be evaluated by OPR in the adjudication of the captioned matter. It is requested that the following be addressed in your response (Douglas Factors):

1. The relationship of the alleged offense to the employee's duties and position and its impact on management's confidence in the employee's ability to perform;
2. The employee's past disciplinary record;
3. The employee's recent performance record and reputation within the workplace;
4. The notoriety of the offense within and outside the FBI or its impact upon the reputation of the FBI;
5. The clarity with which the employee was on notice of any rules that were violated or had been warned about the conduct in question;
6. The potential for the employee's rehabilitation;
7. Mitigating circumstances surrounding the offense, such as unusual job tensions, personality problems, mental impairment, harassment or bad faith, malice or provocation on the part of others involved in the matter;
8. The division's recommendation as to the appropriate range of disciplinary sanctions applicable to the employee's conduct.

This recommendation is optional. Absent a recommendation, OPR will determine final disciplinary action based on existing policies and established precedent. In the event that OPR conducts the investigation, OPR will submit the results of the investigation to your respective division for input. If your division's recommendation is not received by the BUDED OPR will determine final disciplinary action based on existing policies and established precedent.

Receiving division is reminded of guidance set forth in prior Director airtels to all ADICs, et al., entitled "Delegations of Disciplinary Action Authorities to ADICs and FBIHQ Division Heads," dated 2/23/94 and 1/30/95, in which it is noted that no administrative action may be taken with respect to employees under your supervision in OPR investigations unless expressly authorized by OPR, upon OPR's receipt and review of the investigative results of the inquiry.

Provisions of the Privacy Act (Title 5, US Code, and Section 552a (k)(5)) govern this investigation. Please be alert to the fact that the interviewee's identity and information provided might be released to the subjects of the inquiry. No promise of confidentiality should be made to FBI management officials or Agent or non-Agent supervisory personnel who are asked to furnish information concerning an employee under their supervision. The interviewee should be cautioned, however, that his/her identity and the information provided may, pursuant to certain administrative inquiries or judicial proceedings, be made available to the subject of the inquiry if the information is used, in whole or in part, to support an adverse personnel action.

In conducting an OPR inquiry involving personal relationships, the following should be adhered to, as stated in Part 1, Section 1–21.2 of the MAOP: "It is not intended that an administrative inquiry will involve an unreasonable intrusion into the private lives of FBI employees. These inquiries will be pursued only where there are indications that the conduct in question impacts upon work performance and/or the ability of the FBI to discharge its responsibilities."

Whenever feasible, OPR inquiries will be structured to avoid exploring romantic or intimate relationships if other factual issues will resolve the inquiry or if a general acknowledgment of the relationship sufficiently establishes the offense. Although OPR investigators need not negotiate with a witness or subject over the information to be provided they should explain the relevancy of the information being sought. OPR's ability to compel responses, even when the questions may be personal or embarrassing, carries with it an obligation to ensure that the questioning and the documentation of the employee's statement are as respectful, discreet, and dignified as is consistent with establishing all the relevant facts impacting upon FBI operations and the performance of the FBI's mission.

Division management should be cognizant of the significant stress often placed on an employee who becomes the subject of an OPR inquiry and be sensitive to the mental/emotional state of that employee. Upon presentation of the OPR Notification Form, the subject of the inquiry should be provided with an Employee Assistance Program (EAP) informational brochure with the name(s) and contact number(s) of their division's EAP Representative(s) listed. If the facts of a specific case reasonably indicate that such measures are prudent, appropriate steps should be taken to afford counseling for the employee under the provisions of the EAP, or other means, to ensure that the employee's concerns are appropriately handled. In especially sensitive or obviously stressful situations, consideration should be given to having an EAP counselor present immediately following the interview of the employee.

**Documents and/or reports prepared during the course of this investigation must not be uploaded into the Automated Case Support (ACS) System until advised to the contrary by OPR. Should the division find it necessary to set forth leads to other divisions, those divisions should be advised of this restriction.

LETTER FROM ADMINISTRATIVE SERVICES DIVISION DATED OCTOBER 24, 2003, CONCERNING USE OF INDEFINITE SUSPENSION IN PERSONNEL MATTERS:

An indefinite suspension is defined as the placing of an employee in a temporary status, for an indeterminate period of time, without duties or pay pending an investigation, inquiry, or other agency action. An indefinite suspension may be imposed when it is determined that an employee's continued presence in public may be detrimental to the FBI's operations, or national security interests, pending additional investigation into the underlying conduct of the employee.

On 11/22/1994, policy was implemented allowing an employee to be placed on administrative leave when his/her Top Secret (TS) clearance was suspended during the initial stages of a security investigation and indefinite suspension when the TS clearance was revoked. This policy further provided that an employee could be placed on indefinite suspension in certain cases involving suspected criminal conduct.

The Department of Justice and the FBI have been tracking the use of administrative leave and noted this form of paid leave extending for periods exceeding one year on occasion. As a result of this review, the below-described policy changes are being implemented for all FBI employees (excepting members of the FBI Senior Executive Service who are governed by the adverse action provisions set forth in separate policy).

New Policy—Indefinite Suspension based on Suspension of TS Security Clearance

When an employee's TS clearance is suspended, written notification forms the specific basis for the suspension. The SPM's decision to suspend a TS security clearance will trigger action by the ASD to prepare a letter, signed by the Personnel Officer, advising the employee that he/she will be placed on indefinite suspension (without pay or duties) and the reason for such action.

In the letter, the employee will be advised that he/she may elect continuous use of accrued annual leave, compensatory time off, or sick leave, if appropriate, rather than being placed on indefinite suspension. Any request for sick leave can only be approved by the Personnel Officer, ASD. When accrued leave is exhausted, no advanced leave will be granted. The employee would continue on leave without pay until the clearance is restored or revoked. If the employee chooses this option and his/her clearance is later restored, the leave he/she used cannot be restored per government regulation.

Every attempt will be made to ensure that the letters from the SPM and Personnel Officer are delivered to the employee in tandem, unless circumstances dictate otherwise. These letters will be transmitted to the employee's division head for delivery.

New Policy—Indefinite Suspension based on Revocation of TS Security Clearance

Any employee whose security clearance is revoked will not be given the option of using leave. When an employee's TS security clearance is revoked, the employee will BE PLACED ON INDEFINITE SUSPENSION. If the employee is already on indefinite suspension from the initial security clearance suspension, no further action will be necessary.

New Policy—Criminal Conduct

Should the Office of Professional Responsibility (OPR) find that reasonable cause exists to believe an employee has committed a crime for which a sentence of imprisonment may be imposed, a letter signed by the Deputy Assistant Director (DAD), OPR, will be prepared advising the employee that he/she will be placed on indefinite suspension (without pay or duties) and the example, by an indictment, arrest, the filing of a criminal information, credible news reports of egregious acts that are detrimental to the Bureau's mission, such as murder or national security offenses, or through a judicial determination of probable cause. A warrant-less arrest alone may not be sufficient to establish reasonable cause. Separate action may be taken to suspend the employee's security clearance in connection with a criminal case. In these types of criminal conduct cases, employees will not be given the option of using leave.

Right of Preference Eligible Employees

An indefinite suspension for more than 14 days considered an adverse action under Title 5, United States Code (USC), Section 7512 and Title 5, Code of Federal

Regulations (CFR), Part 752.401 (a) (2). When an adverse action is proposed or taken against a preference eligible employee, i.e., certain veterans or the spouses, widows, or mothers of veterans who meet the definition of "preference eligible" in 5 USC Section 2108, specific statutory rights apply. Information regarding these rights will be contained in the letter from the Personnel Officer or DAD, OPR, advising the employee of the proposed indefinite suspension.

Since federal law requires that a preference eligible employee continue to be paid during the advance notice period even if required to be absented from the work place, any preference eligible employee receiving a letter proposing his/her indefinite suspension will remain on administrative leave with pay until a final decision regarding placing the employee on indefinite suspension is made and communicated, in writing, to the employee.

New Policy—Change to Non Preference Eligible Notice and Appeal Rights

ASD will prepare and/or approve indefinite suspensions in cases involving the suspension of TS clearances and will continue to handle those involving the revocation of TS clearances. OPR will prepare and approve indefinite suspensions in certain cases involving criminal conduct. Effective this date, ASD and OPR will advise in the written notice of indefinite suspension to non-preference eligible employees that the indefinite suspension will be effective upon receipt of the letter.

Although there is no statutory or regulatory requirement, current FBI policy allow a non-preference eligible employee to appeal an indefinite suspension to the Assistant Director (AD), AASD. Such appeals are not deemed to be productive since the indefinite suspension is contingent upon whether a presence in the workplace will be injurious. If circumstances change due to facts uncovered during the investigation, the need for continuing the employee on indefinite suspension is considered at that time. There, effective this date, ASD and OPR will no longer afford appeal rights to non-preference eligible employees being placed on indefinite suspension.

Outside Employment

During periods of indefinite suspension, an employee may request approval for outside employment following established Bureau procedures, which include review to determine whether the proposed outside employment presents a conflict of interest. For a field support employee, an outside employment request should be submitted through the security officer in the field office where located. For an FBI Headquarters support employee, an outside employment request should be submitted to the Reinvestigation Unit, Security Division. For a Special Agent, an outside employment request should be submitted through the Employee Benefits Unit, ASD. Form FD-331 should be used for such purposes. Review will be expedited upon the employee's request.

Unemployment Compensation

The written notice of indefinite suspension will include instruction to the office to provide the employee a copy of Standard Form 8, Unemployment Compensation for Federal Employees (UCFE) Program; Notice to Federal Employees About Unemployment Compensation. For additional information on this topic, employees must contact the state or local unemployment compensation office.

Termination of Indefinite Suspension

Indefinite suspension ends when a final decision is made based on the results of the investigation. If the employee's return to work is dependent upon restoration of the employee's clearance, that employee is immediately eligible to return to a paid status following such restoration. In each such case, the Assistant Director, Administrative Services Division will cause a review of the circumstances to determine whether back pay may be appropriate for the period of indefinite suspension and make decisions on a case-by-case basis. In addition, when an employee's return to work is delayed, back pay may be afforded from the time of the decision to allow the return to work and the actual return to work date. Such cases are reviewed on their merits and decisions regarding pay and placement are made accordingly.

 Manual changes follow.

Appendix 3

Portions of letters sent from the Special Agent Advisory Committee (SAAC) to the director in July 2002 concerning the selection and operation of management.

> *Although every Agent is familiar with exceptions to this view, the Agent managers who are well-respected are just that—exceptions. With the current practice of providing advantages in consideration for FBIHQ supervisors for the artificially-designated "non-stationary" field desks, Agents with little real case experience or accomplishment are often given assignments as field supervisors, responsible for an entire squad of Special Agents. At the field level, a supervisor with inadequate and relevant case experience can bring the productivity of an entire investigative program to a screeching halt and severely damage Agent morale. Although it may seem counterintuitive, specific case experience becomes less important the farther from actual casework and Agent manager rises.*
>
> *To quote the findings [of a recent study] Agents across the board expressed reluctance to become involved in a management system which they believe to be hypocritical, lacking ethics, and one in which we lead by what we say and not by example. Most subordinates believe, and most managers agreed, that the FBI is too often concerned with appearance over substance. Agents believe that management decisions are often based on promoting one's self interest versus the best interests of the FBI. It is a little*

disconcerting that "most managers agreed that the FBI is too often concerned with appearance over substance." Agents believe that this should not be blithely accepted by the FBI's leadership, which is the only entity within the Bureau capable of changing what can only be viewed as a systemic ethical lapse.

The letter went on to state:

The administrative overhead involved in the work of a field supervisor is daunting to say the least. From frequent documentation of file reviews, even in big cases in which the supervisor frequently interacts with Case Agents and others, to inspection papers, program write-ups and "crime surveys" used to determine pre-ordained office priorities, and the documentation of any and everything regardless of how meaningless, this job is often a bore. The regular inspections themselves are often an exercise in minutiae, in a meaningless and collusive process (supervisors are often inspecting those who can and do play a role in their future advancement). There are so many meaningless rules, which are impossible to comply with, that everyone is perpetually in violation. The average police sergeant in most any city and town can often do more with a telephone call than most FBI supervisors backed by voluminous and duplicative documentation.

To add to the frustration, supervisors who attempt to deal with personnel issues such as non-performers, incompetent employees or alternatively "go to bat" for their Agents to get necessary resources, etc. are on their own. These supervisors can easily be viewed as troublemakers who are "creating a problem." The lack of support from above is often dispiriting to those managers and the lesson is not lost on those who might have aspirations for advancement.

The other side of this is that the Agent's job, while also overburdened with meaningless administrative overhead, is often rewarding and even some fun. Agents enjoy quite a bit of autonomy and freedom, certainly in comparison with those in supervisory positions.

Edwards Brothers Malloy
Thorofare, NJ USA
March 20, 2013